Stoicism

Developing a Stoic Mindset for Mental Clarity

(Step-by-step Guide to Reduce Stress, Become More Resilient and Live a Happier Life)

Archie Rooney

Published By **Darby Connor**

Archie Rooney

All Rights Reserved

Stoicism: Developing a Stoic Mindset for Mental Clarity (Step-by-step Guide to Reduce Stress, Become More Resilient and Live a Happier Life)

ISBN 978-1-7771996-8-5

No part of this guidebook shall be reproduced in any form without permission in writing from the publisher except in the case of brief quotations embodied in critical articles or reviews.

Legal & Disclaimer

The information contained in this book is not designed to replace or take the place of any form of medicine or professional medical advice. The information in this book has been provided for educational & entertainment purposes only.

The information contained in this book has been compiled from sources deemed reliable, and it is accurate to the best of the Author's knowledge; however, the Author cannot guarantee its accuracy and validity and cannot be held liable for any errors or omissions. Changes are periodically made to this book. You must consult your doctor or get professional medical advice before using any of the suggested remedies, techniques, or information in this book.

Upon using the information contained in this book, you agree to hold harmless the Author from and against any damages, costs, and expenses, including any legal fees potentially resulting from the application of any of the information provided by this guide. This disclaimer applies to any damages or injury caused by the use and application, whether directly or indirectly, of any advice or information presented, whether for breach of contract, tort, negligence, personal injury, criminal intent, or under any other cause of action.

You agree to accept all risks of using the information presented inside this book. You need to consult a professional medical practitioner in order to ensure you are both able and healthy enough to participate in this program.

Table Of Contents

Chapter 1: The Philosophy Of Stoicism 1

Chapter 2: The Structure Of The World And The Position Of Man 16

Chapter 3: The History Of Stoicism 25

Chapter 4: Marcus Aurelius.................... 37

Chapter 5: Recognize And Manage Stress 55

Chapter 6: The Fine Art Of Tolerance 71

Chapter 7: Part Of A Greater Whole 87

Chapter 8: The Stoics' Origins A Short History 101

Chapter 9: Stoic Philosophy Principles . 120

Chapter 10: Integrating Stoicism Into Modern Society 143

Chapter 11: Material Possessions 168

Chapter 1: The Philosophy Of Stoicism

As already cited, the philosophy of Stoicism goes lower back to the Stoics. The word Stoa comes from the Greek and approach some aspect like colorful corridor, which turned into the call of an ancient portico in Athens at that factor.

There arose around the 12 months three hundred BC. The doctrine of Stoicism, simply in addition to figuratively the doctrine of the Stoa. The Hellenistic fact seeker Zenon of Kition is taken into consideration to be the founder. In the following chapters, have a look at exactly what the instructions he created say, and studies the maximum essential matters approximately the basics of Stoicism.

FUNDAMENTALS OF STOICISM

In order to apprehend what Stoicism is all approximately at its center, the basics of Stoicism have to first be described to you.

Stoicism has lengthy past via a few changes over the years and has showed to be very changeable and adaptable (a particularly splendid function in assessment to many fantastic doctrines, a number of which have end up obsolete).However, the center elements of this philosophy have normally been preserved and characteristic handiest been changed to the amount that the point of interest has yet again shifted to at least one place or each different.

These center regions of Stoicism draw at the regions of physics, common sense, and ethics. Physics is all about the cosmos and the entirety it incorporates. Logic deals with cognitions, factors and proofs. Finally, ethics is directed toward human life. It office work the very middle of Stoic philosophy and in particular the focal point of later teachings.

In the Stoic worldview, the entirety arises on a primordial hearth called the aither. And every substance, i.E. The entirety that exists within the international, has been animated thru divine cause. This divine motive is the commonplace feel simply stated. In this manner, the whole lot in Stoic coaching seems every materialistic and pantheistic.

Pantheism manner that a few shape of divine being is one with the universe. It therefore exists in its entirety, its production and its form and every being is energetic via it. So, there may be no independent personified God. The divine being is one with the arena, discovered anywhere in it and incredible in it.

To the Core of Physics

The area of physics is all about the things of the cosmos and its composition. Understanding and being able to offer an cause in the back of the activities and phenomena of nature and the entire cosmos are essential beginning points of physics.

Stoicism moreover assumes that each one sports are strictly causal, i.E. There is a courting a number of the purpose and impact of an event. This strict causality manner an entire causal chain. This in flip technique that the entirety that happens within the global is due to a formerly taking location causal gadget. If Stoics do not find this causal chain, they anticipate that human cognition is really now not enough at this problem.

The man or woman is likewise decided through a destiny called Heimarmene. Heimarmene is Greek and already represents the embodiment of inevitable fate in older Greek mythology. And need to the man or woman ever oppose his very own predestination, then this too grow to be determined via his destiny.

This idea changed into, and however is, perceived with the aid of numerous philosophers with especially differentiated ardour. In considered one among his works, the British fact seeker Bertrand Russell, for instance, judged this doctrine of causality as an opportunity disparagingly and criticized the truth that this sort of predetermination makes virtuous moves seem useless.

Because in case your private destiny is predetermined, then it makes no distinction whether you behave virtuously or now not.

Other Stoic philosophers, together with the Frenchman Pierre Hadot, saw the freedom of the character as though present inside the Stoic doctrine of causality and attributed a huge scope to it. Hadot claimed that man may additionally want to achieve every other universe via his capability to talk. What is meant with the aid of that is, actually a form of 2d degree from which he can look at topics.

In this universe, as he known as it, causality want to now not attain fulfillment. In this universe, meaning and ethical price need to remember as an alternative. Through this revel in and thru moral values, humans have the possibility to independently divide sports (due to destiny) into the sorts of proper and terrible, so he can charge them. This fee, to which humans can ascribe sports and movements, is the give up result of moral values. However, the questions of man or woman freedom of motion in addition to moral obligation appear again and again inside the philosophy of Stoicism.

The Greek truth seeker Chrysippus of Soloi, who's regarded as one of the most important early representatives of Stoicism, also noticed in the man or girls's inherent ability for cause as a way of analyzing and evaluating activities and the scenario.

Man is ready not to follow an inner impulse blindly, but to decide with the resource of imagination whether or not or not the motion produced with the aid of the internal inclination is good or lousy. As a result, he is also capable of deliver in to her or reject her. In addition, now not only the movement of the person or the thoughts on which the selection is primarily based might decide whether or now not or not some detail must be considered applicable or awful.

Rather, the internal nature of a few different character would additionally be decisive. The inner being of every man or woman, in his contemplation, is a form of herbal superb inherent in the bargain and living issue in the world. Thus, regularly best in aggregate with this herbal first-rate, a person's motion can cause some detail splendid or some issue horrible.

A well-known instance of Chrysippos on this context is that of the rolling cylinder: If a person hits a cylinder on a slope, then he might also certainly offer an impulse for the movement of the cylinder, but the reality that the cylinder will roll down the slope uncontrollably is as tons as her inner beings.

Were it not for the roller's inherent tendency to roll down uncontrollably, then bumping the roller might have a one of a kind effect. If the roll z. B. Steerable, lighter, angular or maybe immobile, then the mere nudging of people might now not cause them to do a good buy damage.

So, the same movement in combination with a one among a kind inner being could have very precise consequences or maybe no outcomes in any respect. Only in affiliation with the natural texture of a reel is the plot likely to be rated as awful.

According to Chrysippus, this inner being is likewise decided thru destiny. A reel will constantly have the assets of rolling. That is their future and their logical content material material fabric.

To the Core of Logic

Logic inside the Stoic revel in offers with language and reason. In this context, specific judgment therefore includes the guidelines of wondering and arguing in addition to the ones of expressing concept via language. It forms, so to speak, a framework for the regions of physics and ethics, the latter may be mentioned in extra element below. Logic encompasses 3 areas: epistemology, dialectics and rhetoric.

Knowledge transfer is likewise spoken of inner epistemology. The epistemology includes now not satisfactory the popularity of things or truths, but additionally the verbal exchange of this records. However, good judgment does no longer simplest talk of herbal popularity, however moreover of putting in place requirements in line with which you could apprehend or installation truths in any respect.

One can also communicate of understanding right here. In this context, knowledge technique creating a assertion whose truthfulness can be installation. In Stoicism, one initially is primarily based on what you may understand with one's senses. However, because it become identified in in advance times that sense perceptions are limited, the Stoic teaching does now not rely honestly in this. Rather, what is identified as proper is what is obvious immediately or after the software of one of the installation necessities.

If some factor should be possible, then this additionally way that the person has so that it will make self-controlled and truely suitable selections. As a end result, those who fail to do that and rather allow themselves to be guided thru the use of inner urges or instincts will now not be able to installation truths. The person who wants to find truth need to truely have the capability to differentiate opinion from fact. A person who is best managed by way of manner of instincts and feelings is not able to this in any respect, and consequently cannot make any honest statements.

So fine someone who is privy to self-control can understand. Language is the medium for spotting and conveying knowledge. For this motive, the Stoic philosophers completed numerous studies on grammar and advanced the number one language teachings. This become the incredible way they'll - to come back returned lower again to physics - display the causal chains wherein they believed with out gaps.

In addition to epistemology, dialectics (from the Greek, to German approximately the artwork of communique), the art work of current dialogic speech, and rhetoric (from the Greek, to German about the paintings of speech), the era of suitable talking in non-stop speech, have been developed and expert. The dialectic in Stoicism is directed in the course of a logical quit.

She is devoted to finding the fact and securing expertise, specializing on the only hand in deductive reasoning and on the other hand in the formal commonplace sense and language of mathematics.

The presentation of arguments and truths passed off, specifically thru specific language manner, amongst specific matters through the in particular regularly used conditional assertion if...Then or thru the causal declaration because of the fact.... A sentence within the conditional announcement examine a few factor like, "When it is day, then it's far light.". The sentence as a causal announcement would possibly consequently take a look at, "Because it is day, it's far mild.".

Finally, rhetoric served to bypass on what come to be received as records in a powerful, established and language-aesthetically attractive shape. This paintings is also essential to many one of a kind areas of philosophy. Overall, however, a touch more emphasis modified into located on dialectics in Stoic training.

To the Heart of Ethics

The vicinity of ethics is prepared the combination of man into the nature that surrounds him. This, from the Stoic point of view, is guy's primary future. This additionally consists of identifying what to do and what no longer to do, with the beneficial resource of the given mind and being.

Man himself has the capability to suppose, to achieve knowledge. This expertise come to be considered the first-rate proper and the epitome of a glad and successful existence. For this, it become vital to benefit self-information and to accumulate intention-promoting behavior and attitudes. One's non-public reason is the method of desire to show the manner there.

This path to self-improvement come to be truly as important, a motivational motive because the natural intuition for self-renovation. And finally, the peace of mind that is obtained at the forestall is also a motivation that the stoic sages already possessed. The so-referred to as stoic sage is seemed due to the fact the right photograph of stoic ethics - he lives in perfect concord with nature and his movements display the four high-quality virtues of stoicism to the identical quantity: knowledge, bravery, moderation and justice. You could have a look at greater about those virtues later.

So, to gain this knowledge modified into the very last reason. In order for this to be triumphant, the Stoics believed, one dreams a strong developed have an impact on manipulate in order not to have interaction in unreasonable moves. In this way you can although loose oneself from passions, exercising frugality and learn how to be imperturbable. This is the center to which present day usage of the term stoic calm refers.

While these days this is often associated no longer most effective with serenity, however despite apathy, passivity, almost apathy, this modified into no longer the case at the time. A Stoic truth seeker summed up Stoic indifference within the following terms: Work as is exceptional for the network. So, one have to do the work in a way that blessings the network without being unhappy or pitiable. What is also splendid about the Stoic coaching is that their know-how of network included every person and did now not essentially exclude any outside cultures.

Although, as an instance, at the equal time as there have been nevertheless spatial borders to the barbarian peoples, they had been in no way consciously excluded from the theories of the Stoic doctrine. When we referred to the network, that meant: the totality of each person and all subjects in this universe.

Chapter 2: The Structure Of The World And The Position Of Man

The worldview of the Stoics has already been touched upon in brief. In this monetary catastrophe, the facts of the vicinity view of the Stoics must be deepened a bit.

Stoic philosophy believed in the eternity of the cosmos, however now not inside the eternity of the earth. All subjects on this planet were ensouled by using way of a shape of divine being, therefore some element divine moreover is dwelling within the good deal. Man is consequently not a specially exalted being or perhaps more crucial than a few thing else in the world - there may be some aspect divine about him, but no greater than all specific herbal things.

Every man or women has a predetermined destiny from which their function derives, similar to the whole thing else in the global. In precept, all topics on this planet are identical. At the equal time, the Stoics divided all entities into properly and lousy, coaching that one must stay virtuously.

Despite an innate destiny, the Stoics believed in human unfastened will. For the Stoics, future referred only to outside tendencies, not to a person's internal life. Those entities not challenge to human will, collectively with existence and shortage of life, poverty and wealth, fitness and illness, fortune and misfortune, and lots of others., have been taken into consideration impartial entities.

Since those had been unchangeable and a part of all and sundry's future, human beings ought to in reality make the awesome of the given situations and now not stay on being irritated approximately the activities or the like. On the opportunity hand, the whole lot that is issue to the human will, have become considered to be assessable and because of this divided into the types of correct and terrible deeds, virtuous motion and unvirtuous movement.

DEATH IN STOICISM

Dealing with dying is likewise a critical and feature aspect of Stoicism. In the more youthful Stoa, the view modified into specifically held that the area is the artwork of a divine principle, this is, a rational precept within the Stoic feel. Inevitably, the whole lot that is glaringly internal her have emerge as moreover a part of this rational art work - which includes bodily demise.

It changed into truly a regulation of nature, part of worldwide affairs that could not be omitted. The expiry of every item have become irrevocably decided as short as it become created. In the identical manner, the death of every residing being modified into irrevocably decided at start.

One of the most well-known and usually repeated Stoic questions changed into: What does it rely how lengthy one avoids what's inevitable? If something is going to show up besides, then there can be no want to spend some time brooding over it and fearing it. At the same time, the Stoics of the younger Stoa moreover identified that the essential repression of dying became also meaningless. Instead, lack of existence need to neither be actively feared nor (probable moreover out of worry) repressed. Rather, it need to be taken into consideration and normal as a natural necessity.

In the Stoic doctrine, fear of 1's private loss of life and mourning for folks who had already died had been just such instincts and illogical feelings that one had to conquer as a manner to attain peace of thoughts. Conversely, if dying does not purpose disappointment or worry, then it's miles now not a problem. However, this argument best lets in folks that are really absolutely immersed in Stoic philosophy.

At the equal time, lack of life emerge as now not seen as the opposite of life, but rather as a part of a near connection among the two. It changed into stated that in case you lived well, you may die properly. For an top notch lifestyles, the duration of lifestyles is not important. Rather, the decisive problem is that the lifetime is used sensibly. The bottom line is that the real Stoic is aware about the knowledge of loss of life but faces it with calm and equanimity.

Whether the human soul is immortal or now not, as a substitute, has been considerably said in Stoic coaching. There are statements with the useful resource of some philosophers that the soul is extinguished with the shortage of lifestyles of the body. In addition, unique philosophers claim that the soul lives on, is purified, receives some element almost divine or similar. A uniform statement for the whole Stoicism is therefore now not to be decided.

THE 4 VIRTUES OF THE STOA

The doctrine of the Stoa is characterised via 4 important virtues, which might be moreover known as cardinal virtues. These virtues are bravery, moderation, justice, and—likely most importantly—cognizance. They had been cited earlier than and can be tested in extra element on this economic damage.

Bravery

Bravery, first and crucial, manner perseverance. Anyone who can persevere in a tough scenario regardless of being at a disadvantage is referred to as courageous. This functionality is commonly related to believing in nice values and moral ideas and drawing the strength from them to rise up for them or even combat, although the scenario appears nearly hopeless. Those who're courageous are inclined to bear a conflict situation despite the fact that there is no assure of their very very personal integrity, freedom, or maybe survival.

Moderation

Moderation is likewise frequently called prudence. It describes the functionality to rein in drives or affects and at the manner to maintain them in a top notch stability. Not surrendering simply to instincts or inner desires, however as an opportunity making prudent or considered and logical picks is at the coronary coronary heart of Stoic philosophy.

Justice

Justice is a complicated virtue and once in a while hard to outline. In principle, justice is the identical old for human motion. As a simple rule, it became regularly written that "identical will be treated further and unequal unequally". However, the query of what's to be appeared as identical and what's to be seemed as unequal in man or woman instances has again and again encountered issues.

Justice inside the Stoic revel in requires a advantageous experience of equality. Certain simple ideas, which incorporates dignity or freedom, are identified equally for each person. The stoic righteous recognizes the equality of people as essentially herbal and therefore as logical.

Wisdom

Wisdom is probably the maximum vital and suitable specific function in Stoicism. It is based totally mostly on a deep information of all connections in nature, the cosmos and existence. The sage has the ability to stand challenges and problems with coherent and logical answers. He exhibits sizable answers to almost all questions without being added about via manner of personal feelings or drives.

It is likewise critical that the selections of the clever normally show to be substantial in the long time. It can therefore furthermore arise that taken into consideration certainly one of his insights isn't always identified as sensible thru others at the begin, considering the fact that they're themselves triggered thru feelings or affects. In retrospect, but, they too will perceive these findings as correct or appropriate and logical. The attainment of wonderful expertise is the remaining intention in Stoicism.

The so-called Stoic sage perfects all four cardinal virtues. However, he is referred to as the stoic sage. The immoderate price of facts is made clear with the beneficial aid of this by myself. In Stoicism, existence as a whole, is consequently regarded as a mastering way in which those virtues are to be observed out and completed.

Chapter 3: The History Of Stoicism

Stoic-based philosophy has changed at some point of the previous couple of centuries, albeit not straying too far from its middle factors. This doctrine of virtuous serenity have end up founded, as already mentioned, for the duration of the one year three hundred BC. In Greece. Find out greater about the historical improvement of Stoicism and the ancient beyond of the commands beneath.

HISTORICAL CONTEXT

The time across the 12 months three hundred BC, turn out to be a time while Greece and its previous teachings and policies were in an unsure characteristic. For a long time, the so-referred to as polis, the state association of historic Greece, commonplace the idea of order and shape.

The polis modified into characterized via the usage of using political and social norms and classifications, but fell into a shape of disaster inside the interim. The boom of the Kingdom of Macedonia shook many vintage structures, which, but, made the time propitious for cutting-edge worldviews. During this time, not satisfactory Stoicism developed, but moreover the lessons of the Epicureans, a philosophical training moreover rooted in Greek. It shared the search for salvation with Stoicism, but understood satisfaction as the high-quality appropriate and the pursuit of it because of the reality the common foundation of human life.

Stoicism then superior into three mainly incisive streams over the direction of approximately six centuries. These streams are genuinely known as Ancient Stoa, Middle Stoa, and Younger Stoa. Today, but, one most effective unearths whole works from the so-called Younger Stoa. The works of the preceding currents are quality partially comprehensible.

The length of the so-called center Stoa starts offevolved offevolved offevolved with the emergence of Greek way of life in what emerge as then the Roman Empire. This merging introduced approximately a partial mutual have an impact on of every cultures.

The Stoic philosophy changed into basically steady with the political actions of the Romans, and so it located its area in some predominant circles of the Romans. The fact seeker Panaitios, who lived spherical a hundred eighty BC. Become born, and have grow to be considered one of the maximum vital links some of the Stoa and the Roman life-style. He tailored the strict separation of spirit and frame (in which the body changed into taken into consideration as disparaging as compared to the spirit) that to begin with prevailed within the doctrine of the Stoics and henceforth defined it as a unit.

In his training, this team spirit long-established the expression of the overall individual. He additionally now not targeted on the unconventional suppression of inner urges, but widely talking on controlling them thru one's non-public cause and moderation. Panaitios moreover diagnosed individual predispositions and imprints springing up via the course of lifestyles. This, in flip, intended that the requirements for living a existence in concord with nature and in keeping with one's very very very own destiny have end up some aspect personal. As a stop end result, in his opinion, the duties of the character will also be decided more in another way.

For Roman way of life, this meant that the responsibilities of the nobility can be fundamentally unique from folks that the Stoic doctrine done to the decrease commands. Through this opportunity of differentiation, the Roman rulers can also take pleasure within the Stoic doctrine.

Over the years, those revised views of the Stoic doctrine had been persisted and in part expanded thru different philosophers.

The Greek logician Poseidonios eventually based totally his personal university of philosophy on the concept of this teaching, in which the well-known Roman flesh presser and orator Marcus Tullius Cicero additionally attended his lectures.

In later instances, as the Younger Stoic evolved, the teaching centered more and more on concrete ethical stressful conditions. However, the Roman Empire did not make this development particularly easy, due to the reality the recognition of the Stoic doctrine fell and rose with the respective rulers, their peculiarities and personalities and the temper inside the public.

This philosophy must have a specially strong effect below one emperor and already lose plenty of its popularity via the reign of the following. Especially under the rule of Emperor Nero, who reigned from 54 to sixty eight AD, the Stoic doctrine came below developing stress. Conversely, Stoic philosophers have been an increasing number of crucial of the Roman emperor.

These philosophers both died early or were exiled. However, they continued their teachings there, now and again even founding their private schools. It was no longer unusual for them to benefit new fans and hand down their wondering to numerous generations. However, those traditions often brilliant took place via the spoken word, in order that these days no longer many teachings can be discovered.

One of the maximum crucial present day Stoic teachings is that of the previous slave Epictetus, which focused on the motif of freedom. In this sensehowever, freedom was now not the abolition of slavery, however a freedom that every person ought to accumulate, no matter whether or no longer or no longer he became a slave or an everyday citizen.

According to his education, all subjects may be divided into commands: those that are genuinely inner one's energy and people which might be beyond one's control. The first elegance consequently includes all such matters which may be related with one's personal actions or the omission of actions. This moreover consists of your very private thoughts, judgments, and dreams. The second category consequently included the whole lot that is unchangeable, which includes one's own body shape or bodily health, social standing and additionally death.

The Stoic way to knowledge, he taught, became to apprehend the primary subjects as values and the latter as morally detached topics. In his opinion, one need to now not task oneself with things which can be indifferent, due to the fact in the end one cannot trade them.

About 30 years after Nero's reign, the Stoics' status in the Roman Empire rose all over again. After all, the Roman Emperor Marc Aurel himself became appeared as one of the most vital representatives of the younger Stoa. His self-reflections are considered the closing considerable testimony of Stoic teaching. The ruler characteristic of the emperor modified into conventional in his coaching as future and as a obligation to the Roman human beings.

In the period that discovered but, Christianity rose to grow to be the us faith within the Roman Empire and the Stoa lost its rank and recognition as a cease give up result. However, there were inclinations in Christian schooling that absorbed and merged with Stoic worldviews of ethics and morals. Remarkably, the Stoic philosophy had a strength on the Christian faith. Not satisfactory that, the Stoa moreover endorsed Islamic perception in a comparable way.

In the overdue Renaissance (at some point of the 15th and 16th centuries in Europe), so-referred to as neo-stoicism in the end superior. This shaped well-known and well-known thinkers, because of which the lines of the Stoic teachings endured to spread. The moral philosophy of Immanuel Kant, who is recognized for his philosophy throughout the Enlightenment (spherical 1700), became additionally drastically inspired by means of the Stoa.

After all, the Stoic philosophy additionally has an enduring effect on our gift. This may be seen, as an example, in requirements of psychotherapy in the USA and in political-philosophical discourses on ethics and morals. Even if we use stoic pretty often in cutting-edge parlance, for those who actually seem calm or relaxed and are no longer lovers of the vintage doctrine, there are despite the fact that representatives of this philosophy in our society.

FAMOUS STOICS AND THEIR VIEWS

To get a higher evaluation of the severa Stoic methods and developments, right right here are a number of the maximum crucial names in Stoic philosophy. Maybe one or the opposite appeals to you and also you would really like to address their private development in greater detail?

Panaitios

Panaitios is one of the maximum vital Stoics of the center Stoa. He is also regarded as one of the most vital links among Stoic education and the Roman life-style of rulership. In his education, the formerly strict separation of thoughts and frame changed into changed and the whole organism was now regarded as a unit. His coaching additionally focused more on the improvement of reason and moderation and much much less at the natural suppression of instincts.

It have become furthermore Panaitios who centered greater on private traits and character variations of the character and because of this located the predetermined destiny with reference to the character. This resulted in the unique duties for wonderful human beings, in order that e.G. B. The emperors and rulers may also moreover want to regard their duties greater as a company to the humans, but additionally as a unique predestination.

Poseidonios

Poseidonios have emerge as moreover one of the most important Stoics of the middle Stoa. He persevered the classes of Panaitios and advanced them even further. He went on long research trips for his teachings and for that reason broadened his horizons like on occasion every extraordinary philosopher did. The famous truth seeker Cicero, who later wrote down the instructions of Panaitios and Poseidonios, moreover sought out his personal college of Stoic coaching.

Epictetus

As already cited in "Historical Context", Epictetus have become one of the maximum vital philosophers of the Stoic doctrine. Epictetus lived in Rome as a slave for a long term, but changed into then expelled from Rome and based his private college of philosophy. He came into touch with the Stoa in Rome. However, Epictetus himself did no longer write any writings, so his teachings have been composed simplest via the written traditions of his disciples.

Epictetus targeted on ethics in the Stoic teachings and, similarly to the herbal philosophical teachings, furthermore at the sensible implementation of this philosophy. In Epictetus' training, a stricter difference is drawn than in advance than among subjects which is probably past one's non-public strength and subjects that you could change via one's very very own strength.

Chapter 4: Marcus Aurelius

Marc Aurel emerge as no longer handiest one of the most powerful exponents of Stoic philosophy, but furthermore a Roman Emperor for nearly twenty years. He is one of the most crucial representatives of the more youthful Stoa. Especially inside the final years of his lifestyles, Marc Aurel wrote the most vital writings that belong to the Stoic philosophy. He spent most of these years inside the challenge camp. There he wrote, amongst different subjects, his self-reflections, which from modern-day day angle belong to the so-referred to as worldwide literature.

The team spirit of phrases and moves became especially crucial for the teaching and philosophy of Marc Aurel. Whatever have end up idea, said or taught had to be positioned into movement. In his philosophy, then, the Stoic technique of getting to know finally of life and usually doing all of your excellent is of splendid significance. It did not depend how lots changed into taught and studied, as long as the path of lifestyles end up directed towards being constantly virtuous and attaining records. Ultimately, his philosophy is likewise formed with the aid of the reality that Marc Aurel himself needed to deal with severa strokes of fate and became confronted with imperial stressful conditions that had to be solved. These difficulties of his very own life and getting via them customary his philosophical thoughts quite.

Seneca

You can also furthermore have heard or examine about Seneca earlier than analyzing this ebook - and this call will certainly accompany you in your similarly route. After all, he's one of the maximum well-known philosophers. Seneca became one of the representatives of the younger Stoa, however now not simplest a truth seeker, however moreover a baby-kisser and naturalist. He have emerge as mentioned, specially for his appealing speeches, which unfortunately had been out of place because of a loss of written documentation.

Although he preached Stoic frugality and moderation in his teachings, he have emerge as himself one of the wealthiest and most influential men of his time, and for a time even an consultant to the Roman Emperor Nero, in spite of the reality that the Stoic duration of his rule have become considered certainly one of droop and uncertainty professional. This, in flip, caused the Stoics to shift their lives increasingly more within the route of solitude.

This retreat from the general public international meant that the lovers of the Stoa contemplated increasingly on their very non-public internal being and located even extra rate at the perfection of the internal being and the attainment of records, and plenty a good deal less and lots much much less on outside values, u . S . A . Or political powers and, societal goals.

While this retreat turn out to be visible as voluntary and almost preferred with the beneficial useful resource of a few philosophers, in Seneca's education it have turn out to be visible as some issue critical, ensuing always from the brand new manner of lifestyles of domination, so that you can maintain pursuing the Stoic lifestyle. This manner of life have turn out to be increasingly focused on the cardinal virtues and the mind-set with which things and sports inside the international had been considered. Under Seneca, the Stoic doctrine modified into for that reason shifted increasingly to the focal point of ethics.

Although Seneca tried to steer the emperor significantly, he changed into not very a achievement and turn out to be ultimately accused by way of the use of Nero of being part of a conspiracy towards him.

Ultimately, this even precipitated Nero ordering Seneca to take his personal life, which he emerge as compelled to do. During his time as an consultant to Nero, his movements as a politician did not continuously seem to be totally according with Stoic teachings, which in detail brought him grievance from exceptional Stoics even all through his lifetime.

Seneca taught vital versions in some relevant areas of the Stoics. Already in the antique Stoa a difference have end up made among 4 first-rate forms of humans: the clever, the knowing, the silly and the ignorant. The final intention became continually the attainment of statistics, but at the same time as inside the teaching of the vintage Stoa, handiest this was valued as a very precise success and purpose. Seneca already noticed superb fulfillment in having set out at the direction there.

The classes as such out of place some of their place in Seneca's coaching and the crucial steps and approaches obtained in importance. The first and most critical step for Seneca became looking. In his opinion, the choice to decorate one's personal self could not be discovered, and but it come to be the number one essential step in the commonplace technique.

Seneca changed into furthermore increasingly more aware that hardly ever everyone will obtain attaining the very extraordinary purpose, absolute understanding and unshakeable thoughts-set. The technique of attempting will become all of the more big. Seneca additionally an increasing number of taught modesty and frugality, explaining that due to the reality that every person is born terrible, wealth cannot be a herbal proper and therefore no longer a few element that people ought to try for. In order to stay on, minimum gadgets have to suffice – further to no longer having to starve, die of thirst, freeze to death or die in a few different manner.

You can already prevent this with minimum objects and so that you need to be grateful and content fabric, so long as you have were given a roof over your head, a blanket for bloodless days, sufficient to eat and drink. Seneca additionally cautioned that the ones who've extra than that create themselves days of fasting and poverty and, for a quick time period, relearn a way to make do with the naked requirements. That way you will simplest definitely learn how to understand what you've got greater.

One need to moreover detach oneself from prosperity extra often and examine not to emerge as dependent on it. According to Seneca, anyone who makes themselves depending on prosperity and fabric goods is without a doubt terrible on the internal, and those who make do with the naked necessities are absolutely wealthy on the inner.

Summary

In addition to the ones stated above, there were of path one of a kind philosophers and teachers of the Stoics, some of whom had been more critical, a number of whom were a good deal much less essential. Not each of them left their personal writings, so sometimes the teachings have not been completely preserved for posterity or had been disseminated underneath the call of one of the university students. The philosophers referred to above appreciably formed the improvement of the Stoic doctrine in one in each of a kind techniques. Knowing and know-how them is surprisingly endorsed in case you want to research greater about Stoicism for your self. You can of route spend more time with the ones people and the records of your coaching if you desire, but the examine given want to already display beneficial.

Stoicism in Everyday Life - Theoretical Overview

So now the historic past and center factors of Stoic philosophy, how can you are making Stoicism your way of existence? What does it suggest to be a Stoic in regular existence in recent times? In this a part of the e-book, discover ways to placed the idea of Stoicism into workout for your existence!

In regular existence, stoicism sincerely approach bringing a positive serenity, calm and equanimity with you. Equally crucial is not letting your temper rely on events which may be inevitable and past your manipulate. And finally, stoicism moreover way letting cause and accurate judgment reach our everyday life and in big thing turning off internal dispositions and drives.

This way, among wonderful subjects, that topics that you cannot have an effect on yourself, e.G. B. Praise or criticism, you need to now not have an effect on your emotional kingdom. You cannot determine and trade whether or not your fellow human beings address you in a friendly or impolite way, so that you need to take delivery in their behavior within the spirit of the Stoa and e.G. B. Don't be shaken thru the unkindness of others. However, the opposite is likewise real: best comments from other human beings must not have an effect to your mood both. On the other hand, you need to continuously be at peace with yourself, glad and snug, irrespective of whether or not a person is tremendous to you or now not.

In order to exercise such conduct and look at it sustainably, you ought to first analyze and apprehend what matters are for your palms and what aren't. Many of the events of our regular existence are based totally on numerous factors, some of which we are able to have an effect on and others no longer. Recognizing those as such is an vital prerequisite for a stoic way of life.

An instance of this could be the give up end result of an examination. For each exam you could take a look at long and hard, solve wearing occasions and mentally put together for them. All of this is as plenty as you. Whether you whole the exam efficaciously in the long run does no longer rely entirely on those elements. On the alternative hand, a number of awesome factors which you can not impact additionally play a function. This can e.G. B. Your form at the day or situations that affect it, which encompass the climate, your nation of health, tiredness, ultra-modern-day strain, and lots of others. The diploma of trouble of the questions is also a issue which you can not have an impact on, as is the strictness of the examiners, and so on..

If you take element in a sporting opposition, you can thoroughly impact your education proper here, however victory or defeat does no longer depend on that on my own. Rather, the training and the abilities of the opposition, probable the climate, your every day form, the each day shape of the competition, in all likelihood the assist of the spectators, etc. Play a function. You can't affect any of this.

Of direction, this doesn't advocate that you need to now not make any attempt for your everyday lifestyles from the outset, since you can't ultimately have an impact on the final results of an occasion except. It virtually manner that you ought to shift your goal: in desire to that specialize in winning or succeeding, you need to attention on doing all of your wonderful in the regions which can be yours. And you have to find delight in that.

Some philosophers, like Seneca, additionally cautioned living in poverty for quick durations, or denying yourself small pleasures, in order to admire extra what you've got to your actual life. This doesn't advise which you need to give up the entirety and hit the street along with your tent, but in case you want to attempt it, you can. For instance, you could pass searching out a quick period with little or no coins or consciously forgo candies, television or a lager after paintings on high best days. If you do that on days whilst you definitely experience like having a beer or chocolate, you could discover ways to recognize the little pleasures, all the extra in the end.

Becoming a Stoic – Practical Exercises

Now you've got got were given already located out all varieties of subjects about the ancient past, records and center factors of Stoicism and additionally what it may suggest in regular existence to be a Stoic. Therefore, in the next part of this e-book, we're able to recommend how you can end up a Stoic your self. With the following realistic bodily sports, you can short learn how to positioned into effect the philosophy of the Greeks in your everyday lifestyles and as a give up end result gather extra peace and serenity.

BASIC SKILLS AND CHARACTERISTICS

What number one abilties need to a Stoic very own? You have already take a look at a bit of this in previous chapters. Now permit's skip into a bit extra detail. Read the requirements approximately the capabilities and tendencies of a Stoic to recognize how the sports activities will let you and what you need to recognition on so one can actually come to be a follower of the philosophy.

In doing so, hold reminding your self that some of the peculiarities will now not appear in a single day - counting on your cutting-edge state of affairs, this is a greater or less lengthy-term manner. If you are greater of a non violent and serene individual except, then you can locate some settings less tough.

If, but, you're instead confused and insecure, you'll possibly want a piece extra time. So do not located your self below pressure with the whole lot, however try to supply yourself time and preserve at it.

Remember, all of existence is a analyzing technique.

SELF CONTROL – DEALING WITH INSULTS PROPERLY

Calmness and composure are specifically vital for a stoic thoughts - but how do you in truth stay calm at the same time as a person deliberately (or in a roundabout manner) insults you? Keeping your inner peace in such situations is often not that smooth. Most of the time, on the equal time as someone tells us a few element that we find out offensive, we get indignant.

When a person insults us in the back of our lower again, we often understand it as even worse. And it isn't always uncommon for the spontaneous preference to do the equal to the opportunity character, to pay him once more. Unfortunately, that hardly ever receives us everywhere.

On the contrary, it has a bent to gasoline the ugly temper and in flip triggers the choice inside the different person to be unfriendly to us once more. So, the pleasant element is to find out a way to react in every other manner to insults or unsightly terms. And with a chunk extra experience and workout, you can truely be able to often come to be greater cushty!

Stoicism and its proponents have superior numerous techniques for handling insults. One consists z. B. Questioning if what you have been counseled is in reality authentic. After all, why get upset about some factor that obviously is clearly the case? An example: someone says that your rental looks as if a colorful kid's room.

Instead of having disappointed approximately it, take into account it for a 2nd: Is your condominium clearly colorful and freaky? Do you want them like that? Then it's no longer actually a drama on the same time as someone says the plain out loud. Instead, marvel at the uncommon cutting-edge who believes that you have not already found the thrilled shades in your home.

A 2d technique is to ask who issued the insult. Is it a person you specifically apprehend and whose opinion you fee? Then you could likely take his statement as a hint to enhance or trade something. On the opportunity hand, if the insult comes from someone you do not like and whose opinion you do not fee besides, then you do not really need to care, proper?

The Stoic's 1/three method for dealing calmly with insults is to deal with the offenders as they could with small kids. It must be assumed that practical and realistic adults do no longer insult for no motive. So, individuals who but do some aspect like which can be behaving extra like unreasonable little children. And what character would possibly significantly get so upset at a little one's insult that they get indignant or possibly are seeking out revenge? After all, you comprehend that those small youngsters are though too immature and that you should not join too much significance to this form of declaration.

Another possibility is to take it with humor. This is especially powerful at the same time as you're in direct contact with the man or woman. Just snigger away the insult. Not remarkable does this assist you stay calm, it additionally brightens your temper. Finally, you could discover ways to sincerely tolerate the conduct of others. This is of direction a greater tough depend. However, if you have severely understood the way to place into effect this tolerance, then nobody can damage you anymore.

Chapter 5: Recognize And Manage Stress

Stress also can make everyday lifestyles extra hard for us and thwart our serenity - that is all the more common in our modern normal existence. Hardly everybody nowadays does not war with demanding times, even though they will be super short. Dealing with stress effectively is therefore exceedingly important, so as to find the way to a stoic manner of life. Basically, the sooner you recognize the traumatic situation as such, the easier it is going to be to deal with it.

When you admit that the situation is stressful for you, the next step may be to be sincere about it with others as properly. Talk approximately pressure together at the side of your buddies or family - it frequently allows mainly to get the strain off your mind, so to speak. And possibly your fellow people can also do some of the come up with the results you need.

Sometimes we get forced due to the reality we address more duties than we have to. So do not be afraid to invite for assist whilst it's miles necessary or appropriate. Do you have were given pressure on your non-public life due to the fact you are trying to reconcile artwork, own family, pals and so on? Ask your associate or exceptional own family individuals to do some of the family chores. Do you usually address greater obligations in your professional area than you have to? Ask colleagues to do a number of the offer you with the outcomes you want if it's also their area of obligation. Learn no longer to deal with greater obligations than is crucial and fair.

You also can use different strategies to control pressure and benefit greater composure. It can e.G. B. Assist to take more breaks - or maybe small breaks do amazingly well! Take a wreck of five to ten mins extra frequently and also, depart your desk/place of job or anywhere else you are busy. This permits to easy your head and preserve going for walks greater effectively and productively. Make the exceptional use of the time to get a few sparkling air and/or exercise.

Even if it's just a few minutes, stretch the ones muscle tissues, arise for a coffee, open a window, and lots of others. And most importantly, do no longer punish your self internally on your breaks. Treat yourself to the breaks with benevolence and without a accountable ethical feel. They will do you accurate. If you desire, you may use the breaks to artwork on the practical sports sports on this ebook. Some of those can be done in minutes, anywhere, whenever. This is the manner you kill birds with one stone!

If you often do not feel as lots because the state of affairs, it is able to moreover be a useful method to install writing what are referred to as to-do lists. To try this, break down the huge duties into numerous small ones. Write down steps that you want to complete in sooner or later. The better organized you are, the greater efficient you could work and the quicker the stressful scenario is probably resolved. Also, if you could circulate a few things off the list, it's going to make you experience unique. You will at once experience better and further relaxed due to the fact you may see for yourself what you have were given already completed.

In order to undergo existence with more serenity, you may additionally test your surroundings - are you surrounded with the resource of compelled and burdened humans on a each day foundation? This can have a primary effect on your very very own attitude. So, try to hold reminding your self that the strain and bustle of others ought to no longer be your strain and anxiety. And try and surround yourself with calm and snug humans more often. That can do you masses of genuine.

You'll fast discover that the closer you get to the stoic manner of lifestyles simple, the much less complicated it will likely be to address strain. And the much less complex you control pressure and the calmer you grow to be, the nearer you get to popular stoicism, too. One step comes at a time, however after you get the ball rolling, it gets less complex and much less hard. So, consider your self and strive to analyze a bit bit greater each day.

MINDFULNESS AND ACCEPTANCE

The training of mindfulness has grow to be more famous over the previous few years. Mindfulness describes a country of complete presence of thoughts, just so the surroundings, one's private body and internal existence are absolutely perceived with all senses.

In a state of mindfulness, one does no longer enjoy any distraction from trains of concept, fantasies or daydreams and one is free from judgements. This sort of interest and focus of 1's non-public being and area inside the here and now can be additionally practiced even as meditating. Such sports also are part of the Buddhist teachings, however moreover have their place in the Stoic way of existence.

After all, popularity of all subjects herbal is part of the middle of Stoic philosophy. In order to anchor the stoic way of life deep internal, mindfulness bodily sports may be pretty huge and useful. Such bodily video games may be respiratory bodily video games in that you make a aware try to take a seat or upward push up right now and take deep breaths inner and out. Concentrate most effective in your respiratory and understand it with all your senses. A comparable exercising is called the 3-minute dip. You take a three-minute harm and immerse your self, so to talk, in all the impressions and activities of your modern-day environment.

Just try and be clearly privy to the whole lot spherical you with all your senses. What do you be aware? What are you listening to? Do you scent some thing? How is your body feeling at this moment? Try to soak up the whole lot in as a good deal element as feasible and to understand what is happening or is spherical you at this 2nd. And mainly, attempt not to make judgments.

MINIMIZE NEEDS AND PRACTICE FRUGALITY

Frugality is regularly practiced in Stoicism. Striving for material desires and achievements is not virtuous movement inside the enjoy of Stoic philosophy. Instead, you need to be content material and recognize what you have got. In order to have a look at this, one have to learn how to restriction one's needs - in choice to striving for extra money, a promoting, recognition and so forth, Stoics are content with the cutting-edge situation.

So, try to exercise frugality for your ordinary lifestyles and reduce your goals. To do this, it's miles best to first ask your self the intense question: What do I really need in life? Feel unfastened to preserve in thoughts it for a while and sense loose to jot down down what's clearly critical to you in lifestyles. Ask yourself this question regularly earlier than searching for new client devices.

Do you actually need greater new clothes or do you have already got an entire closet entire? Even in case you want to buy some thing however cannot provide you with the money for it right now, it's far an outstanding idea to significantly ask yourself if the tremendous is actually critical. Do you've got already were given a roadworthy car? Do you really like strolling for your method and in the characteristic you already hold?

Smaller tips and physical sports, which you may get to realize inside the later a part of our e-book, can help to boost those trains of concept. These encompass e.G. B. Gratitude lists and additionally horrible visualizations. Write down what you have got got already got and what you will be happy about. Write down what absolutely topics. And then, if you have that second wherein you honestly crave what you do now not have, select up those lists and mirror on all the good stuff to your lifestyles.

The Greek truth seeker Epicurus of Samos as soon as stated: For whom sufficient is surely too little, not anything is enough. He sums it up very well that people, specially in modern day society, are continuously striving for delivered. There will constantly be some difficulty you do not already have, and once you have got got it you may need some component else. Those who have a simple hobby lengthy for more money. Rich human beings compare themselves to even richer human beings. Instead, commonly preserve in mind what you already have and that this is enough to stay on.

Since there'll continuously be more, striving for this can not supply you pride. Because you could in no way have the whole lot. Only folks who acquire this and discover ways to reduce their needs to what's essential will eventually be capable of be satisfied with what they have got in existence.

SERENITY AND INNER CALM

Serenity and inner peace are some of the fundamentals of the stoic manner of life. However, it is regularly precisely those houses that cannot be placed into exercise as with out hassle as was hoping. However, with a touch exercising, you may fast discover a manner to gradually practice composure.

It's exquisite first of all the beneficial resource of practicing in smaller traumatic situations. After all, our cutting-edge everyday existence is entire of it - particularly when you have a circle of relatives to take care of, are very busy professionally, and lots of others. For many humans it's miles in particular difficult no longer to get disappointed approximately smaller strain factors, as those in fact gather in ordinary lifestyles. Then it isn't always actually the system or family strain that upsets you, but small matters just like the prolonged wait and queuing at the grocery store, searching out a parking region, spilled espresso inside the morning, and masses of others.

One of the terrific techniques to attempt is to try to distance your self from the situation. Learning now not to take topics as non-public attacks can assist in particular.

Most of the little stressors are actually not directed at you as a person - anyways, the whole parking zone or the espresso do no longer care who you are. Also, if a person tries to get in the the the front of you inside the grocery keep, it's rude, but not a few component aimed toward you immediately. In such situations, try to gain mental distance from the situation. Once you have got this underneath manipulate in regular pressure, you'll sooner or later discover it less complicated to address special conflicts (e.G., a dispute with colleagues or within the own family).

By the manner, gaining distance also can propose taking bodily distance. Sometimes you truly need a 2d to in reality physical keep away from the situation, and at the way to can help you relax lots extra. So go out into the glowing air for a second and try and breathe deeply. The bodily approaches, collectively with a quicker heartbeat and quicker respiration, also can go once more to ordinary. Sometimes it furthermore permits to in brief keep away from the character you have been having a controversy with. It's frequently hundreds plenty much less complicated to loosen up and loosen up in a impartial surroundings.

You will see that the greater frequently you exercising composure and calmness in such conditions, the more likely it's miles going to be anchored in your internal attitude.

Apart from traumatic conditions, interesting hobbies can also assist to benefit a cushty inner existence. Start incorporating yoga into your each day habitual and meditate for 5 minutes inside the morning or midnight. Such exercises can paintings wonders in terms of internal peace.

Just because the Stoics often withdrew if you want to cope with themselves and their function inside the cosmos and to mirror absolutely on their internal being, you may also regularly create time for yourself in that you are by myself with yourself and your inner being. This can be an extended meditation or mindfulness workout, or in reality looking at at the night time sky on a clean night.

Philosophize approximately the size of the universe, undergo in mind how small anybody and each problem is inside the massive cosmos. You can have a examine that such time-outs make an terrific difference. Not handiest will your frame near down at some stage in this time and you can furthermore get away the traumatic regular existence, you'll moreover check how such wearing activities and trains of concept will change your internal thoughts-set by an extended way.

Overall, you must now not placed your self underneath stress, however without a doubt try to get time for your self as regularly as viable. After a while, consistent exercise exercises becomes established and also you becomes better and better at assembly the disturbing normal life with comfortable calm.

15 EXERCISES FOR EVERYDAY LIFE

In this section you'll find out a group of bodily games that you may with out hassle include into your normal existence to in addition exercising stoic composure. You do not need to do they all each day, of route, but it's beneficial to duplicate a number of them on a everyday basis. Try the wearing sports one after the alternative and you can without a doubt fast be aware a alternate on your attitude.

The Stoic Morning Routine (Prepare for the Day)

Start the day with a stoic morning ordinary. Many Stoic instructors have already identified that consciously adjusting to the day each morning for a certain term ought to make a large distinction. In the morning, set aside five to ten minutes for a few form of stoic meditation exercise.

It is brilliant to go to a quiet area to try this. This can be your mattress room if not anything distracts you there, or maybe better the lawn or nature. Breathe inside and out consciously and deeply and cognizance on the day earlier of you nowadays. Think about what's going to be important that day, what is going to appear, and don't forget how first rate to respond to the ones situations in a way a good way to make you behave much like the person you want to be.

Also understand and be given that there can be factors that you can't affect. Try to be with yourself as you do this workout. And inform your self that the day can be appropriate.

Chapter 6: The Fine Art Of Tolerance

Tolerating or accepting the matters we can't exchange ourselves is one of the precious arts of Stoic philosophy. It really takes a while to look at the pleasant paintings of tolerance. But you may begin with the aid of manner of telling yourself every day that the arena is whole of factors and sports which might be from your manipulate. And because you cannot alternate things, you actually need to take delivery of them.

You've possibly heard the phrase, Happy is he who forgets what can not be modified. This phrase in the beginning comes from the operetta Die Fledermaus. And but it suits fairly in the context of Stoic schooling. Because there, too, it's far about main an outstanding and satisfied lifestyles without losing your mind and time on what we can not exchange. Maybe the sentence from the bat is less complex to keep in mind in your brain because of its rhyme?

You also can write this announcing on a card and body it, stick it to your reflect, or deliver it to the administrative center and immortalize it in your desk in case you wish. Seeing such sentences written inside the the front of you could be pretty helpful in normal life. Whenever you generally will be inclined to forget about what you desired to look at from the Stoics, you are automatically reminded.

Remind your self as often as viable what number of of things in the international are past our manage - and in addition importantly, how masses of them are beyond absolutely everyone's manage. For instance, dying is a herbal part of each life and no one can have an effect on big natural activities.

And all and sundry will experience things of their lifestyles which might be inside the strength of various people however beyond their reach. Your private moves also have an effect on the lives of others, however often can not be modified by them, clearly so outsiders furthermore want to receive your moves and selections. A comforting idea, isn't it?

You will see that the extra frequently you tell your self that there are topics that you can really simplest obtain, the much less difficult it's far going to be in case you need to address ugly sports in normal existence.

Awareness of the Impermanence of all things

You need to commonly be aware of the impermanence of things. This applies to everything in existence and additionally to life itself. As described earlier, this does not imply that you have to fear demise or the primary impermanence, quite the possibility: you must turn out to be aware of impermanence, acquire it yourself and so, do not worry too much about them.

What is inevitable have to now not weigh down some time with worries and hardships. You have to actively exercising elevating awareness of impermanence, due to the fact it's miles precisely at the same time as you are inwardly involved that you have a propensity to suppress this impermanence.

Regularly reminding your self that the whole thing in lifestyles is brief may additionally moreover even make it less complex in an effort to reduce your desires and exercising frugality. After all, what difference does it make to have extra cash if it's high-quality going to be quick-lived besides? You additionally discover ways to cope better with loss when you have already changed your mind-set to the reality that everything in the international is short. Because in case you are already organized for the fact that the entirety will ultimately come to an surrender, the forestall can be a lot much less surprising and less excessive.

Stoic Aphorisms

Aphorisms are stand-by myself portions of knowledge or mind that encompass simply one or a few sentences. There are a number of Stoic aphorisms that you may recite to your self as regularly as feasible. When you communicate such aphorisms aloud to yourself or write them down, the Stoic teaching will constantly be with you.

You may discover a few particularly powerful fees from famous Stoic philosophers on the give up of this e-book. Use the ones to get began and revel in unfastened to search for more. Maybe write your preferred perception on a small card and stick it to the replicate? So, you examine the concept proper next on your personal pondered picture every morning. Surprisingly powerful!

Learning for a Lifetime

Never forget about that Stoicism is also about persevering with to look at at some point of existence. All of life is directed toward being virtuous, gaining information, and continually doing all of your pleasant. Of course, typically seeking to do your notable additionally way typically looking to enhance your self. There is constantly a few thing that you may but artwork on and there are continuously areas wherein you can nonetheless research more.

Of direction, this isn't to mention that you should be annoyed by way of using this obvious imperfection - pretty the opposite! This is truly to make you conscious that it's miles k if you maintain working on yourself and nonetheless apprehend matters that you have previously left out.

Because that's what existence is all approximately. If all of lifestyles is a getting to know approach, then achieving the top of information and distinctive feature at an early age isn't a purpose or an possibility. Just as the arena and instances are constantly converting, you may, have to and could change and enlarge again and again.

So do not strain if you experience like you are approximately to discover your self in a state of affairs you cannot address but. In life you may constantly have a observe new topics and that is the way it's meant to be.

Self-manage - Don't be Someone Else's Puppet

How frequently an afternoon are you externally controlled via way of others? Do you watched that doesn't arise to you very often? Then reflect onconsideration on it over again and go through drastically and punctiliously how often you are directed through outsiders or exceptional affects in the course of the day.

Who does now not get pulled down through the feedback of others sometimes? And how regularly are we brought on via manner of the use of a few difficulty we see on severa social media channels nowadays? How regularly do commercials and the evaluations and tips of our fellow humans have an effect on us and who has no longer seen their temper plummet because of rain or a gray sky?

External impacts and precise human beings steer us in a certain route hundreds more frequently than we understand or would like to recognize. But being privy to that is an vital step at the way to the Stoic coaching. Try to preserve in thoughts who or what is currently influencing your actions and options or your mood. Feel free to ask your self that greater times a day. And while you apprehend that they will be certainly simply events due to factors outdoor of your non-public sphere of have an impact on, then attempt to shake off the ones thoughts and refocus on what's inside your sphere of have an effect on. Don't be one-of-a-type humans's puppets! Don't permit advertising or what you have got visible on Facebook, Instagram and Co. Manipulate you.

A few examples: Just due to the fact the whole digital global is raving approximately a modern-day automobile could not imply you want one. When you phrase a ultra-cutting-edge product online it virtually is being marketed anywhere, you will likely just want it because it's suddenly been advertised - not because of the truth you actually need it.

Up until this 2d, you did not even apprehend that this kind of product even existed. If you're at peace with your self, why ought to a bit rain ruin your mood? Especially due to the truth your horrible temper may not drive the rain away both. If you have were given supplied a fancy new pinnacle and you like sporting it, why need to it provoke you in case your co-employee would no longer like it?

Try to constantly endure in mind that you are not a puppet to be controlled. You by myself are answerable for your self.

Here and Now

Stoicism is ready the proper right here and now. Everything that comes in the future is inevitable except due to a predetermined destiny, and seeing that the entirety that isn't always in a single's non-public power is logical and natural, one need to usually recognition most effective on the right right here and now or on what you could affect inside the present.

So, in case you discover yourself drifting off into fear about the future or anger about the past, try to deliver your self returned to the prevailing. Because you can high-quality effect them right now. Try to visualise what you may make a distinction within the 2d you're in and bring your cognizance lower again to it.

Of course, that does not recommend that you need to go through life with genuinely no plan all the time and must throw all your mind approximately life overboard. But you need to often remind yourself that you may only have an effect on what's taking area inside the imply time. The beyond is immutable and the destiny isn't yet malleable.

Practice Gratitude

In the Stoic doctrine, one is thankful for what one has in desire to striving for more cloth gadgets. You can workout gratitude very effects in normal life. You can for example, every night time before you visit bed, simply say what you're grateful for that day—or higher however, write it down. Keep a form of gratitude magazine and write down up to three matters every day that you are thankful for. You also can check aloud what you wrote down distinct days to remind your self of it.

Another extremely good concept can be placed within the tale of the farmer with the beans in his pocket: Every day the farmer had a handful of beans in his proper trouser pocket and with every little second of happiness, with every joy, with each precise

2nd he introduced a bean of the proper pocket into the left.

In the night time he counted the beans and belief lower once more to one of the happy moments with every one. Maybe you try a comparable trick from time to time? After all, it does no longer need to be beans. You can use beads, pebbles, coffee beans or anything you may think of. Just deliver it a try. You will simply be amazed at what you can be pleased about within the middle of the night. And even though it's most effective a bean, you can honestly appearance once more at the on the spot with a grin.

Change of Perspective

Changing perspective can artwork wonders. Of direction, it's not usually smooth to region yourself in exceptional humans's footwear so you can surely preserve near their attitude, but you need to try as often as possible. The better you get at it, the easier it is going to be a excellent manner to get a impartial point of view and the composure this is going with it inside the subsequent step.

In order to change mindset, you want to noticeably ask your self: How is the alternative character viewing this situation? This isn't always usually clean, particularly in struggle conditions, however it could be in particular effective. If you find out it particularly hard at the beginning, you could also ask the opportunity individual to gently describe his/her view of things.

Take a second to understand and permit the factors sink in. The extra you attempt, the much less complicated it'll ultimately be to get a cutting-edge attitude. In order to teach this extra intensively, you could also adopt a very remote places attitude. Gaining a impartial view of things can help to provide events in a completely extraordinary and, in particular, unbiased slight. You can discover greater about the impartial mind-set or objectivity inside the subsequent problem.

Sometimes the Stoics moreover talk approximately taking the so-known as hen's eye view, i.E., the top view. Try to look at the conditions, first rate subjects or virtually short periods of your lifestyles like a spectator from above. If you've got been a being who really watches everything from afar, how would probably you feel about it? If you had been to have a take a look at comparable happenings in masses of different places at the equal time, would not all of them seem small and nearly unreasonable?

Objectivity

Objectivity is one of the most crucial elements of regular Stoic existence. Freeing oneself from one's very personal emotions and evaluations of factors and activities within the international is a first-rate paintings. Nevertheless, with a touch time you may workout objectivity. At every opportunity, attempt to take a look at things and activities from a independent attitude. The formerly mentioned change of attitude can be the first step on this path.

Once you discover ways to take a contemporary attitude on the sector round you, a independent attitude may additionally emerge as easier. Because the advantages of things that you for my part apprehend as terrible, or the disadvantage of what you apprehend as excessive pleasant. A impartial attitude way spotting that the whole thing in lifestyles lets in for more than one views.

In the begin, you could frequently remind your self that the whole thing that takes place and exists in the international has a logical connection from the Stoic component of view. The mindfulness physical sports activities also can let you nice apprehend things in area of comparing them. At least as quickly as an afternoon, popularity on a few component this is taking location spherical you and make a aware try to recognize the situation with out comparing it.

This may be a chunk hard in the starting, however the extra frequently you simply cognizance at the information and now not the feelings involved, the less complicated it turns into. Also, try to adopt an intention attitude greater frequently in struggle situations. To do this, you could really ask yourself the subsequent question: How must an objective or independent observer recognize this case?

Even in case you only take this attitude for a very brief time, you can get superb insights from it. And the better you get at the objectivity perspective, the higher your peace of mind becomes.

Chapter 7: Part Of A Greater Whole

Realize that you too are part of a larger entire. That technique three topics. For one, it method which you are a natural a part of the universe. You belong right right here, you've got were given been given a wonderful destiny (as a minimum in step with Stoic teaching), there are obligations which you want to satisfy, and your lifestyles as a whole is part of a extraordinary remarkable judgment. Don't you found it's far a beautiful and nearly comforting idea?

At the equal time, however, this additionally method that they'll be fantastic a part of a larger ordinary concept. Your life, your moves, and your views aren't any less critical than those of these round you, but they're no more important either. Looking at the entire universe, you're exquisite a very small element. So do no longer power your self too crazy with the small problems of ordinary lifestyles.

For the general view, those are not that essential. Even in terms of your whole existence, a small 2d of pressure is really a trifling detail, isn't it?

Finally - and this might be the most crucial content cloth of this mind-set - it additionally way which you are a part of a larger idea that still consists of every body else and the whole lot else on this worldwide. Think of the universe as a body of that you also are a element. Everything in the cosmos belongs collectively like limbs belong to a body.

So, for this body to characteristic, we need to act and artwork collectively as one. So, try to inform yourself as regularly as possible that you want to not paintings in the direction of your fellow humans - but instead paintings for them and substantially with them. If, as the Stoics taught early on, we are all born of the same nature and inspired with the resource of the usage of the same divine not unusual enjoy, then we are all linked in a unique manner, one may additionally nearly say associated.

It is also from this popularity that the Stoics believe that we need to direct our moves toward the commonplace nicely and live virtuously in a way this is super for society and the arena. This is the handiest way we are capable of lead a outstanding life - additionally for ourselves. Marc Aurel once defined it very aptly as follows: What is of little want to the beehive is of no need to the bees every.

Choose Your Company Wisely

As said underneath the stress management economic catastrophe, the humans you surround your self with can through hazard have an impact on your internal calm or tension. Therefore, you must generally choose your organisation with care. Of path, this isn't always typically your responsibility on my own - you may rarely choose your art work colleagues, nor a few family participants.

But in your free time you need to attempt not to allow traumatic humans pressure you out. If you locate it difficult no longer to be encouraged with the aid of your self, spend the nighttime with friends who've a chilled impact on you. Spend the lunch smash with colleagues who no longer most effective burden you with their very very own paintings worries, however who even have a powerful impact on you and additionally permit the break be a damage. Dealing with calm and snug people will certainly have a exceptional effect on your mood ultimately.

Of course, this does not imply which you need to write off every body who suffers from pressure or anxiety. Instead, on every occasion you may, try to find out company that influences you in a wonderful manner, mainly even as you're confused.

So, if your associate is as an opportunity confused or your pleasant pal goes via a demanding and negative segment, then of course you should not stop spending time with those loved ones proper away - but you may have mutual pals in the middle of the night invite if you want to do you every pinnacle, or discover a today's interest wherein you may meet like-minded and nicely-balanced humans.

Doing Good is More Than not Doing Bad

As already defined severa instances, stoicism has nothing to do with passivity, even though it regularly seems so in current parlance. Therefore, it's also essential to realise that in Stoicism, living well and meaningfully way more than heading off awful topics.

So do not attention your movements on avoiding lousy topics, but as a substitute on actively doing pinnacle subjects. You can effects include this into your everyday existence via way of seeking to live every day in a manner that actively contributes to the exceptional of society. This may be finished thru assisting a super purpose, growing a donation or genuinely being actively satisfactory to colleagues in the administrative center. When making your choices, moreover consciously be aware of this and lightly ask yourself: Was this movement to avoid awful behavior and changed into it truly top behavior?

Still now not quite wonderful what the distinction is? If you pass a homeless person on your manner to art work, there are several possible publications of movement you may take. You may want to probably disparage or maybe insult the homeless person—a terrible act. If you do not, but actually stroll beyond him, then you definately have averted a horrible act. However, that doesn't mean which you have finished a few factor particular with it. If you leave the individual with some small exchange as an alternative or maybe get them a espresso or a small breakfast from the bakery across the road, then you haven't handiest averted the horrific opportunity movement, but absolutely, actively carried out a few detail unique.

If in reality all and sundry in the administrative center is gossiping approximately the brand new colleague, you can each be a part of in, stay out of it, or communicate up or be exceptional to the colleague. So without a doubt due to the fact you stay out of the slander does now not recommend you have executed a amazing deed, you've got simply prevented a lousy deed. If as an opportunity you offer an motive at the back of to the others that you have to chorus from gossip or invite your new colleague for a coffee, then you definitely have actively done some thing super.

Negative Visualization (Anticipating Bad Events)

Negative visualization method which you are imagining very intensely that the worst. The worst-case state of affairs, has already came about—regardless of the worst trouble that could display as tons as you might be.

So, it may be the dying of circle of relatives, your very very own death, painful illnesses, poverty, loneliness, and so forth. Through everyday terrible visualization, you understand how precious what you certainly have (e.G., loving humans, wealth, health, and masses of others.). We often most effective virtually respect it whilst we lose it. So, awful visualization brings our focus decrease again to what's in truth essential to us in lifestyles. This manner you may moreover deliver it the pleasant amount of hobby.

The Stoic Evening Routine (Rethink Your Day)

Just like a morning regular, an evening recurring of schooling the Stoic schooling may be very beneficial. Ideally, you have to try this each day. Don't stress or blame yourself in case you don't be successful, however try to make this exercise a ordinary each day.

Part of this routine is absolutely looking lower again and reflecting at the day. What did you do, assume and say that day? And what of it modified into particular, cheap and in the public hobby? What need to you have got were given carried out higher? Feel unfastened to put in writing down all of this down and mirror on yourself. That is precisely what Marc Aurel did at the same time as he wrote his self-reflections.

He wrote commonly for himself and pondered on his private moves. Today we draw critical Stoic insights and education from this. And it's far feasible which you too will benefit new insights not nice while writing, however moreover in some unspecified time in the future while studying via your very very very own reflections.

Appendix: 5 Quotes to Get you Through Everyday Life

The nice impact of motivating statements have to now not be underestimated. A small impulse is regularly sufficient to remind us what without a doubt topics and what we should focus on. Therefore, right here are 5 vital costs from Stoic philosophy which you want to commonly accompany on your further course.

"IT IS NOT THE THINGS THEMSELVES THAT MOVE US..."

But the views that we've got of them." (Epictetus).

This well-known quote from Epictetus sums up the content of Stoic schooling pretty well. After all, there is an inescapable common sense to the topics and happenings of this global, and rarely is what we sense approximately a state of affairs or thing inherent inside the nature of the component itself.

But how we undergo in mind them and what we remember them affects how we experience, our mind-set. When a tree falls over in a storm, it is no longer the fall of the tree itself that moves our emotions, however whether or not we're glad about it, unhappy about it, or without a doubt gather it as having happened.

"YOU FEAR EVERYTHING AS IF YOU ARE ONLY MORTAL; ..."

You preference the whole thing as in case you have been immortal too." (Seneca).

This quote from Seneca sums up the irrationality wherein we often stay within the great viable manner. How often can we worry about topics because we're essentially aware of our impermanence - no matter the truth that we can't keep away from it. And but most humans strive for cloth gadgets, but moreover for success and other subjects, no matter the fact that in the long run they'll have no which means that the least bit. With this statement, Seneca sums up thoroughly how mindless this manner of existence is.

"THE ATTEMPTS GREAT, IS ADMITABLE..."

Even even though he falls." (Seneca).

With the ones phrases, Seneca testifies that Stoic philosophy isn't always about passive existence, however about spending one's life sensibly and nicely and continuously giving one's brilliant. At the same time, it indicates that achievement and failure are not indicators of whether or not or not a person has spent their existence meaningfully or nicely within the spirit of Stoic philosophy. Nor do these outcomes say a few issue approximately whether or now not or no longer the character is admirable or not, or whether or no longer or now not they're satisfied or sad.

If you do your superb and do no longer waste it gradual with vain matters, you stay in the spirit of the Stoics and do no longer must worry approximately success or failure.

"THINK ABOUT WHAT YOU HAVE..."

Than what you lack." (Marc Aurel).

This quote from Marc Aurel sums it up another time, that in preference to continually striving for extra, you want to be happy approximately what you've got had been given in lifestyles. Worrying approximately what you do not have would no longer make someone happy and there'll always be a few element you do not have (however). Instead, recognition on all the exceptional stuff you've got were given already had been given in existence - your health, pals, circle of relatives, a roof over your head, some thing to eat every day, life as such... Because you're alive! You may be grateful for that.

"YOU ARE FREE TO WITHDRAW TO YOURSELF AT ANY HOUR..."

Treat yourself to this pretty often, this stepping once more into the internal and rejuvenate your self." (Marc Aurel).

The final of our 5 charges expresses in particular strongly the philosophical concept decided in Stoic education: to narrate to oneself, a ways from the thoughts and mistakes of others, far from all that isn't always in our power . Anyone who learns this has understood the training of the Stoa.

Chapter 8: The Stoics' Origins A Short History

Talking to a stoic is like having an in-depth speak on happiness. Stoics see eudaimonia because the very first-class existence cause. What is it, and why does it recall? Simply stated, "eudaimonia" refers to a country of entire and utter happiness. This is a hazy and deceptive solution, but. Achieving eudaimonia in Greek philosophy is growing the proper instances for human happiness. Under this definition, it extends past easy contentment to include morality, distinct feature and having a revel in of route in a unmarried's lifestyles.

Hence, Greek philosophers attempted to decorate themselves via growing to their whole ability. Several philosophers, together with Aristotle, Socrates, and others, noticed this as a critical purpose. Much of Aristotle's teachings center on the idea that eudaimonia may be attained thru the cultivation of splendid characteristic, diligent attempt, and satisfying all the duties one's times and nature impose upon them.

He said that human beings need to be the high-quality they will be in their jobs as dad and mom, physicians, and educators. Each of these humans has masses of greater responsibilities which can be simply as time-consuming and vital to them as their maximum important jobs. More than sincerely being splendid in their most important jobs is needed. They have to reap all one of a kind jobs with a purpose to gain eudaimonia. For example, further to being worried for his or her kids, mother and father might also produce other duties, collectively with furthering their careers or being worried for their aging mother and father.

Apart from the important duties, certainly definitely all and sundry has a purpose in lifestyles, that's what distinguishes people from exclusive animals. Finding and desirable your life's right calling is essential to experiencing eudaimonia. Maintaining composure underneath stress and performing with integrity are hallmarks of sophisticated human capability, yet those trends seem in a extraordinary way in each people.

According to our interpretation of Aristotle's thoughts, eudaimonia encompasses happiness and ethical flourishing, religious accomplishment, and achievement.

As eudaimonia is greater than definitely happiness, happiness is a part of eudaimonia. On the alternative hand, happiness may be fleeting, defined in phrases of pride, and received regardless of the aid of way of immoral way. In assessment, eudaimonia is commonly a everlasting united states of america of the united states of being that can be measured in terms of perfection and attained via essential a virtuous existence.

To achieve eudaimonia, you have to discover ways to stay in concord with nature, alongside facet incredible humans. One key function that units humans apart from unique animals is our capability for logical perception. Stoic philosophy pastimes to assist its followers grow to be extra degree-headed inside the face of extreme emotions (apatheia). You need to moreover educate your self to be unconcerned with what occurs to you within the outside world. Stoicism can be traced lower back lots of years to the eudaimonic beliefs, the pursuit of that first-class, and the strategies for carrying out it.

The golden age of classical Stoicism spans three hundred BC to 2 hundred AD and may be damaged down into the three sections below.

Early Stoa (three hundred - one hundred BC)

As a philosophical motion, Stoicism can be traced lower back to Athens, whose founder, Zeno, hooked up the primary university of idea in 300 B.C. Zeno's views had been profoundly prompted thru Epicurism, a university of philosophy introduced via Epicurus round 307 BC. Epicurism is a expensive-orientated way of residing. Advocates of this way of life sought opulence via indulging in sensual sports activities activities, which encompass consuming and consuming to greater. Later on, its largest rival, Stoicism, rose to prominence.

As taught via Zeno, Stoicism trusted in advance philosophies, most drastically cynicism, which valued simplicity and morality. Modern Stoicism may be traced returned to him, and his theories prolonged stoic philosophy in unique judgment, ethics, and physics. As time went on, Stoicism advanced right right into a philosophy with a more potent emphasis on moral values. Yet, recollect that ethics can't flourish in isolation. It has to make feel logically and physical.

Cleanthes, a disciple of Zeno's, carried at the subculture of Stoicism. While Cleanthes used his personal method of schooling, his lessons had been based totally totally simply at the mind of Zeno. The 1/3 important truth seeker to make a contribution to the development of Stoicism have become Chrysippus of Soli. He is credited for extending and strengthening Zeno's foundation through propositional commonplace revel in. Propositional correct judgment is focused on understanding extra about the workings of the universe and the position of mankind in it.

His teachings emphasised the significance of human freedom in acts and beliefs in selecting your future. Drawing on Zeno's ethical theories, Chrysippus emphasised that comprehending and expressing ethics required know-how of the person of the universe. Despite furthering Stoicism, he additionally emphasized that the human spirit can also additionally additionally brief grow to be discouraged and crushed on the same time as we permit our impulses to trump logical reason. After Chrysippus, different thinkers like Zeno (Tarsus) and Diogenes (Babylon) improved the stoic way of residing, culminating in Antipater's mind (Tarsus).

Middle Stoa (one hundred BC - 0)

By shape of 100 BC, Stoicism had grown big and had traveled from Athens to Rome. Panaetius, whose teachings have been greater flexible than Zeno's, championed stoic philosophy on this Stoa. His lectures emphasised physics in vicinity of reasoning, making Stoicism much less difficult and less complicated to recognize for university college students and professors alike. Panaetius is credited with introducing Stoicism to Rome and growing its facts of Neoplatonism.

Neoplatonism is a collection of ideas that arose and flourished at some point of the Greco-Roman era. It advanced in the end of a time of historical corporealist schools of idea which include Stoicism and epicureanism. It changed proper into a dominating worldview that helped researchers and college college students very well recognise the cosmos and humanity's function in it.

A sort of stoic thoughts and perspectives from diverse instructors frequently define the middle Stoa. This is each different motive why Panaetius determined it less complicated to simplify Stoic philosophy with the aid of focusing much less on common feel and additional on the physics of Stoicism. With the eclecticism in perspectives from diverse teachers, one of the highlights of the center Stoa is that an appropriate of an uncontested, united faculty of Stoicism faded. Despite this, stoic concept remained sturdy ultimately of this era.

Posidonius come to be the second philosopher to similarly Stoicism at some stage in this time, whose views reinforced Panaetius at the same time as aligning with those of Aristotle and Plato. Stoicism turned into regular in Rome after Posidonius, Cato the Younger, and Cicero. Cato, especially, become recognized for his unshakeable ethical integrity and austere way of dwelling, which may be frequently appeared as stoic icons. In hindsight, Cato's conservative teachings were more just like Chrysippus and Zeno's than Posidonius and Panaetius'.

Late Stoa (0 - 2 hundred AD)

The past due Stoa passed off at some level in the reign of the Roman Emperor. Across the Roman empire, this time modified into marked via political and cultural development and growth. Imperial Rome modified into at its pinnacle about 117 AD at the same time as it controlled all from Western Europe to the Middle East. Augustus Caesar modified into the number one imperial Roman emperor, ascending to energy after his exquisite uncle, Julius Caesar, changed into assassinated. Augustus' rule became incredible with the resource of prosperity in infrastructure and jail changes, and he restored Rome to its former splendor thru protecting the town's borders.

Imperial Stoic thinkers centered on ethics in preference to technological know-how and not unusual enjoy. The final Stoa created most of what we realize about Stoicism nowadays. It is in reality really well worth noting that, of the three Stoa, handiest the very last one has specific texts, making it the maximum remarkable time for Stoicism.

The majority of Seneca's works handled moral issues. Furthermore, Arrian's student Epictetus, whose thoughts have become famous because of Arrian's art work, is a super instance. For the best creation to Stoicism, Epictetus' Handbook is commonly suggested to beginners. The life and writings of Epictetus, who became born a slave, educate us loads. His artwork endorsed teachers consisting of Marcus Aurelius and Albert Ellis.

Marcus Aurelius, the Roman Emperor, emerge as probably the most well-known Stoic reality seeker. During his military campaign in Germania, he maintained a pocket ebook known as Ta eis heuton (To Himself), now called Meditations. Many humans have take a look at and been endorsed via his writing, and Meditations is one of the maximum noted pieces of stoic literature. He promoted global citizenship, rationality, and strength of mind, amongst tremendous values in spite of the fact that pertinent in modern-day-day manner of lifestyles. Meditations are generally regarded due to the truth the past due

Stoa's very last good sized stoic literature, and severa researchers and college college students have cited it as an invaluable beneficial useful resource for private growth and development.

It is really worth noting that the past due Stoa is regarded because the maximum extensive in Stoic information thinking about there aren't any surviving works or materials from the early and center Stoa. You may also even take a look at that most of the stoic literature is prepared modern-day intellectuals and philosophers.

Stoic philosophy has developed through time to come to be a undying way of residing, valuable to many human beings looking for which means in their lives. Stoicism offers route and reason in existence for buyers, emperors, sportsmen, or leaders. The important mind of Stoicism, as taught with the aid of the use of manner of Zeno inside the historical Stoa, have remained unchanged and function precipitated the teachings of philosophers which incorporates Epictetus and other teachers to these days.

Stoic Philosophers

One of the principles of Stoicism is that everyone may achieve greatness. Your history must not be a difficulty. For example, historic Stoic thinkers got here from some of backgrounds. From a slave to the emperor, they all opted not to allow their beyond or present to determine their lives or destiny. The stoic philosophy that ruled their lives become some factor all of the thinkers had in not unusual. Whatever conditions, hardships, and tribulations they confronted, they observed to attention on what become inside their manage. They changed the direction of humanity via furthering stoic standards via that specialize of their ideas, deeds, and mind alternatively of outside forces outside their manage.

Each of the important philosophers can be delivered in short in this phase. Take phrase that every had fans and disciples, maximum of whom left no legacy. This is due to the fact devices and texts from their technology have in no way been decided.

Marcus Aurelius

Marcus Aurelius is the most well-known Stoic leader. Although born into an rich family, many human beings did not expect greater youthful Aurelius to upward push to the region of Emperor of the Roman Empire. He modified into passionate about searching, boxing, and wrestling. When his reign ended, Emperor Hadrian chose Antoninus as his successor and charged him with adopting and fostering Aurelius to be successful him. With Antoninus' death in 161, Aurelius began out his reign.

Throughout the subsequent a long time of his reign, Aurelius faced some of challenges, at the side of conflicts with barbarian tribes to the north, the Parthian Empire, the unfold of Christianity, and plagues that killed off a big a part of his population.

So, why is Marcus Aurelius blanketed on this list? He possessed big authority and come to be likely the area's most powerful leader. He must have become everything he favored if he had wanted to. Like most preceding rulers, he had the choice of controlling the empire at his amusement, high-quality his emotions and appetites, and succumbing to temptations. The reality is that nobody alive may additionally want to have avoided him from performing some issue he preferred.

Several leaders earlier than him had been corrupted with the useful resource of absolute authority, and we had visible many exceptional and promising leaders lose the plot once they ascended to prominence. This have end up now not right of Aurelius. He dedicated his life to establishing his worthiness of authority. The Roman Empire have grow to be large and sturdy, but a smart and ethical emperor additionally led it. Unsurprisingly, Marcus Aurelius is regarded due to the fact the ultimate of the Five Excellent Emperors.

Marcus differs from many beyond and modern worldwide leaders in virtue and intelligence. His pocket book is filled with critiques and teachings on embracing intelligence, justice, and morality whilst resisting temptation. Meditation, a personal diary, is one of the satisfactory reference assets for humility, ethics, self-actualization, private strength, and willpower.

Seneca

Seneca (Seneca the Younger) changed into born in Southern Spain, no matter the truth that being a scholar in Rome, and grow to be the son of a prominent Roman creator, Seneca the Older. He committed his lifestyles to politics, running his manner up the ranks to come to be a reputable economic clerk. His recognition was tainted, however, on the equal time as Emperor Claudius banished him to the island of Corsica in forty one AD on accusations of adultery collectively with his niece.

While in exile, Seneca wrote to his mom to console her. Years later, Emperor Claudius' companion, Agrippina, who could ultimately supply start to Emperor Nero, secured Seneca's launch certainly so he might probably train and advocate her son. Seneca's man or woman is from time to time a deliver of opposition, considering that Emperor Nero went right now to end up an notorious dictator. Believing that Seneca changed into plotting his loss of life, Nero had Seneca completed in sixty five AD.

The existence of Seneca, from the time he come to be exiled to Corsica till his dying, become whole of upheaval, but he in no way wavered from the stoic beliefs and teachings he had evolved. Seneca official Cato, however Attalus was his first and maximum influential trainer. Seneca determined useful lessons approximately riches, religion, sorrow, power, and lifestyles via the adversity he endured.

Epictetus

One of the motives Stoicism is so exciting is that everybody may additionally learn how to stay with the beneficial aid of its tenets with the useful resource of searching at the lives of the most well-known philosophers. Marcus Aurelius, whilst he died, became the remaining emperor of the only empire ever. Seneca modified into an crucial figure in the Roman Empire because of the fact he cautioned the emperor. Epictetus commenced out life as a slave. If you study approximately extraordinary stoic thinkers, you may see that Stoicism's impact become no longer limited by way of way in their social repute. The training of Stoicism are conventional, and they'll help everyone locate peace and serenity in every satisfied and unhappy instances.

Epictetus modified into born right right into a rich circle of relatives in Hierapolis, but he changed right into a slave. Epaphroditus, his grasp, allowed him to examine everything he desired, even liberal texts, wherein he sooner or later came into stoic philosophy. Musonius Rufus changed into his direct teach and guide. Freedom from Nero's rule allowed Epictetus to spend nearly a long term training Stoicism at a few level in the Roman Empire. He endured this until all philosophers were expelled from Rome with the useful useful resource of Emperor Domitian, at which detail he escaped to Nicopolis. As time went on, he installed a faculty of philosophy and taught there till his loss of existence.

\

Chapter 9: Stoic Philosophy Principles

Cicero frequently considered Rome's notable orator, first used the phrase "summum bonum" to refer to the best tremendous. Pursuing the excellent correct is treasured to the stoic way of lifestyles. In stoic idea, one-of-a-type characteristic supersedes all one-of-a-kind values. The stoic manner of lifestyles is based totally completely on reacting and behaving virtuously. Virtuous behavior is the location to begin for incredible results, although confronted with stressful conditions, fears, pains, or apathy. The virtuous are rewarded with love, honor, prosperity, reputation, and pleasure.

Virtues related to Stoicism, which includes the "4 cardinal virtues of Greek philosophy" and a focal point on residing in concord with the herbal global. Several definitions and perspectives on stoic tremendous function have developed during time. Ancient philosophers used the term "specific characteristic" to consult an admirable amazing in a residing being. In addition to following the law, the translation furthermore includes striving for excellence. Next, we are going to take a better have a look at stoic developments.

Stoic virtues

The historic Stoics liked succinct lists that would be without problems remembered. Here, we are going to speak approximately the 4 cardinal virtues, which appear on many such lists. During Stoicism's information, its 4 tenets had been related to a completely unique animal logo. The term "tetramorph" describes complex mixtures of 4 one-of-a-kind factors. It emerge as derived from the Greek terms tetra (four) and morph (shape). Hence, the subsequent is the tetramorph of the four cardinal stoic virtues:

Man of understanding

Bill or ox of temperance

Eagle of justice

Lion of fortitude

As you need to examine all 4 tenets in case you want to be taken into consideration in reality virtuous and honest in your acts and intentions, amazing characteristic is the very remarkable true in stoic concept. That's about as best as human nature receives. In special phrases, virtuous person lives as a whole lot as their full human functionality with the beneficial resource of growing the developments that get them proper admiration.

If this is correct, then the sole accurate is that a clever guy is virtuous. Virtue and honor want to moreover be immoderate fantastic. Good deeds and thoughts help us flourish as humans and recognize our capability. We learn how to fee reality and are searching out information due to Stoicism's guiding beliefs. As a society, we are chargeable for treating every body with fairness and compassion, regardless of whether or not or no longer we understand them or now not. Be courageous and educate yourself to conquer and manipulate your fears earlier than embracing power of will and controlling your passions and wishes.

Wisdom (Phronêsis)

The key to a fulfilled life is gaining statistics. Knowing the difference amongst proper and incorrect is a key factor of facts, and it's miles this understanding that ultimately effects in contentment. By records, you're making informed judgments about what to do and what now not to do.

In idea, all of the stoic virtues are strategies to use expertise in decision-making and behavior. Stoics maintain in thoughts recognition the pinnacle of exclusive characteristic as it gives the essential factor to distinguishing amongst what is ideal and what's awful, and what's unbiased in any given state of affairs. It's all about clean reasoning, the important thing to appreciating what certainly subjects in our worldwide.

No time spent on this international can make up for a loss of notion. You want now not be stoic to look the risks and losses associated with indifference. Stoic statistics, rather, specializes in accepting goodness for what it's far. Once you understand that data is the best suitable, your moves replicate that know-how.

Wisdom, in everyday living, is likewise the capability to make feel of the sector round you. There are many sports if you have multiple apathetic preference. You, the stoic, react or select out at such instances via considering what is maximum important. You need to learn how to decide your situation and take the right steps earlier.

Philosophy, now and again called the "love of information," expands on this stoic quality. The wisest route of action is the handiest you pick out now. There is always a lag some of the time you're brought on to behave and while you in reality do so. There is knowing within the time and distance amongst an possibility and on the equal time as you make a decision a way to react to it. In this situation, facts might be visible as an opportunity. Finding that starting is the hardest thing for everybody. If you are taking advantage of that 2d of reflection, you could avoid performing rashly and rather take a look at the precepts of stoic philosophy. Applying philosophical insights to ordinary existence is the essence of knowledge.

Temperance (Sôphrosunê)

Temperance teaches you to maintain your feelings in take a look at. There is a focal point on gratification and leisure on the coronary heart of this unique function. Many have long long gone down in flames because of their disability to rein in their desires for pride. Learning strength of will approximately one's own pleasures, sorrows, and goals is at the coronary coronary coronary heart of this stoic one of a kind feature.

Irrational behavior might also end end result while one allows their desires and pleasures to take over their life. You push aside what's right in choice of what offers you pride at the time. Again, we see how age brings perspective and awareness. Temperance is also worried with personal freedom. It's all about area and strength of mind if you're a stoic. You need not put up to authority on the way to act morally. It may help if you practiced internal area to discover achievement.

When confronted with a desire among what appeals to your emotions and what's morally accurate, you should strike an low value stability amongst your thoughts and impulses. Temperance, therefore, refers back to the condition in which you not best pick out what to do however moreover exhibit prudence in making that preference.

Temperance is more than simply electricity of will or region. It is also about being greater self-aware. The concept of mindfulness or a robust ethical compass may also help you are making sense of it. Lessons on strength of mind educate us to use purpose within the face of temptation. Choosing to behave on your goals ought to be encouraged by means of using a revel in of morality.

Although others can also experience occasions as a whole, a stoic thoughts-set includes disconnecting from them as a manner to allow for aim assessment and depiction. In many methods, it resembles scientific experimentation. Taking a unbiased, nonjudgmental stance lets in one to get a extra whole expertise of a situation in place of only a superficial one. By postponing your judgment, you may allow move of prejudice, greed, and worry. By freeing you from risky attachments or feelings tied to outdoor stimuli, developing past desires and anxieties lets in you to make realistic judgments.

Temperance encourages you to recognize and personal certainly what's vital. The stoics use the allusion to hundreds. Self-control and moderation are synonymous ideas in stoic idea. It isn't always quite masses self-control approximately worldly property however additionally harmony and discipline within the face of fulfillment or failure, pride or struggling, reward or contempt. The transient person of pride need to now not define your happiness, nor need to the fleeting nature of grief damage your happiness. Temperance teaches you a way to avoid the ones volatile extremes.

If you truly do not forget it, a splendid deal of the entirety we do, assume, and say is superfluous. Getting rid of the useless offers you peace of mind and similarly free time. You learn how to do fewer subjects better.

In any situation, the maximum vital query need to be, "Is it crucial?"

Courage (Andreia)

Fear does no longer flow a brave individual. Having courage teaches one to keep in mind in oneself. Knowing the truth approximately an trouble boosts your self warranty in handling it. Thus, braveness is not simplest about going via your fears; it additionally way understanding as loads as feasible.

Courage, one of the maximum primary stoic virtues, can also moreover mean extra than truely bearing physical ache and suffering. Stoics regularly disapprove of cowardice due to the fact it's far the antithesis of bravery. There is in no way a time at the same time as you may find the cash for to lack bravery. You need to have that shape of braveness to your coronary heart whilst developing a risky desire and for your thoughts if you have to determine between some difficulty terrible and some detail terrifying.

Temperance is a not unusual associate of courage. Both need you to have the energy to address your emotions and pressure you to confront your fears and dreams head-on. There is, consequently, a link a number of the 2 traits. You are recommended to overcome your concerns and persevere through hard situations at the identical time as appealing for your better judgment to reduce bad desires.

Nothing that the stoics do not forget virtues can exist apart from some desire or fear. It will help in case you preserve these factors beneath control. Even the maximum high-quality and high-quality stoic want to reveal braveness and temperance. Stobaeus says that bravery is the functionality to differentiate amongst awful subjects and people that aren't and act as a result. Courage additionally involves being robust for your selections. A smart desire is the satisfactory form of desire clearly worth being robust about.

Justice (Dikaiosunê)

Every day, you hear of people pursuing justice all at some stage in the globe. The phrase "justice" has currently been given a crook and literal interpretation, that could be a departure from the particular stoic which means that. For Stoics, justice is prepared more than certainly the law; it is also approximately having straightforward and wonderful interactions with the humans to your lifestyles. Such traits may be tested in a determine's unshakable devotion to their children or in the steadfastness that honors one's non secular beliefs. There isn't always any stress on you to do it, but you recognize that doing so is probably morally commendable. If we take a step another time, we see that justice is in the end about doing what's right, upholding moral requirements, and being a excellent citizen.

The foundations of Stoic justice have been compassion and fairness. While fairness and honesty do no longer appear to have anything to do with the literal definition of justice, it is through the practice of these developments that justice ultimately triumphs. As a social precise function in its broadest feel, justice involves showing kindness and compassion to the ones in need. It is ready social equality, equity, and following the regulation.

Doing what is proper, now not high-quality for yourself but for all of society, is what justice should be approximately. It is probably easy to experience which you do not degree as an awful lot as others or that you don't get sincere treatment in life. If you're aware about those discrepancies, you have to avoid taking any steps that would make contributions to their endured perpetuation. Every element of a stoic's existence need to be achieved with civility, equity, and objectivity.

Marcus Aurelius ranked justice due to the fact the paramount stoic distinctive feature. When it comes all of the manner right down to it, having the braveness that completely advantages oneself is pointless. What applicable is your information in case you need assist to make use of it?

Genuine freedom and contentment come from cultivating the four cardinal traits listed above. The tenets of the Stoic university advocate for readability and directness at the same time as rejecting complexity, hubris, and ambiguity. Stoics apprehend they cannot exchange the arena, however they'll act justly, accurately, temperately, and courageously in reaction to some thing comes their way.

While you can permit the unpredictability of lifestyles paralyze you or set yourself loose, bear in mind which you have a choice. The only manner to have this form of independence is to be virtuous. Even within the direst times, you could commonly make the maximum sensible selection. Follow your wonderful feature and usually do the proper element. That's the restriction of your have an effect on. The relaxation will appear because it should through its sheer nature, without or with your permission.

Disciplines of Stoicism

Stoic philosophers taught about the threefold disciplines that must lead your lifestyles further to the four cardinal virtues. Disciplines of choice, motion, and agreement. Among the Stoics' founding ideas is the idea that one should domesticate braveness and temperance to advantage a balanced, smart, and honest life. You'll want to understand your very very personal desires and apprehensions to do that. One of Epictetus's most well-known tenets, "endure and surrender," emphasizes this identical factor. You need the braveness to appearance your darkest nightmares unfold and the electricity of will to reject your baser impulses.

Discipline of Desire

As a non secular practice, reputation of one's future is one of the education taught with the resource of the place of desire. It's approximately taking a philosophical view of life and embracing your lot as inevitable. This university of concept integrates non secular and philosophical perspectives to sell living in concord with the universe and its population (or, in stoic theology, the gods).

The challenge of desire facilities almost at the crucial one-of-a-kind function of braveness. Self-control is a talent you need to extend, especially regarding your illogical emotions. Also, it might help in case you exercised staying strength to hold your calm inside the face of worry. The capability to control or reject volatile or illusory desires is critical for the stoic.

Your purpose in life should now not be to manipulate the path of sports to make matters move the manner you spot them; instead, it need to be to just accept some aspect comes your manner and bypass on with out resistance. Accepting your future does not advocate which you need to come to be a doormat for certainly absolutely everyone else's troubles. This exercise want to be the cornerstone of your stoic way of life as it prepares you to accept the inevitable randomness of life's occurrences. It teaches you to make the maximum of it slow and alter to some thing conditions existence throws at you.

Don't try and outrun your issues with the aid of manner of going some unique area. Deal with them head-on and get hold of the pain they may purpose. Any unsightly sensations, which incorporates tiredness, starvation, pain, and so forth, are to be expected. They remind you that worry does more harm than what you are frightened of. But it's vital to take into account that no amount of courage can justify unstable conduct. When know-how is missing, courage is irresponsible and dangerous.

Consider a criminal as an example. They need to have the center to interrupt into your place, thieve, or damage you. They haven't any worry, can cope with hassle, and be successful. Yet a crook's courage is focused on achieving evil ends. Justice and knowledge have to result in Stoic courage.

The stoic unique function of temperance teaches its practitioners to control their feelings and keep away from more to pursue justice and expertise goals better. You get the potential to area low price constraints in your wishes. Many people's lives are ruined with the beneficial resource of overindulging. Yet, the concept of strength of will ought to be super from the proper. When individuals exercise restraint and surrender one form of delight, they'll pass overboard with every different.

Good and cautious strength of mind is what is needed. A stoic's thoughts-set inside the route of pleasure is one in each of indifference. It might help if you learned to forgo the things that almost all of humans need at the manner to dedicate your self to doing what is proper and practical. That's how you can use the famous area to direct your actions.

Discipline in Action

Ethical conduct is a prerequisite for fulfillment in the motion task. You can distinguish amongst accurate and evil and feature a enterprise draw near of indifference in your every day sports. The number one reputation of this academic subject is the vending of universalistic values like Stoicism and compassion. It's about locating purpose and following your bliss whilst helping others.

The Stoics believed that distinctive characteristic have become the most effective real appropriate and that it modified into sufficient in and of itself to attain eudaimonia. On the other hand, moral stoics want to teach themselves on the darkish detail of human nature, which incorporates its dangerous impulses, irrationality, vices, and opposing precise characteristic. You need to be aware about them to distinguish most of the coolest and the horrific.

The exercise of this artwork instructs its college students in the paintings of communal coexistence. This suggests that your intention in lifestyles is the prosperity and pleasure of your fellow guy and that you actively are searching out to express this intention through your moves. The most you may do for someone else is to want them well and assist them in some thing way you may; you do no longer effect their happiness. As a stoic, you do your notable inside the entirety you do, but that the good or horrible results are past your manage.

Be deliberate approximately the whole lot you do, and ensure it serves humanity's extra benefit. You ensure the emotional and physical health of human beings round you are a priority, definitely as you may ensure your very non-public is. You enlarge the scope of yourself-like to include helping exceptional human beings.

Discipline of Assent

A key lesson of Assent is the fee of using motive in ordinary conditions. Elements of epistemology and psychology are protected in stoic common sense. Searching for know-how is treasured to epistemology, a branch of philosophy. An epistemologist is someone who studies the motives, reasons, and commonplace experience at the back of sports. After an epistemologist has completed their research, they'll be better located to present an cause of why a splendid occasion will arise, given all of the instances. Mind and behavior are the topics of intellectual studies, which incorporates each overt and covert highbrow approaches.

According to the preceding, acquiescence is a topic that teaches its adherents the way to stay a very good life with the resource of accepting and operating with their private inherent rationality. That's why it is so vital to constantly behave rationally and consist of the fact in all you are saying and do.

This exercise is set up to statistics as it relies upon on successfully know-how who you're. The focus proper right here is to your private vicinity considering expertise who you're at your middle guarantees that you'll typically be targeted. By coming to terms with yourself-reputation, you may test extra approximately your ideals, perspectives, and the basis for your very very own judgments. Your abilities and know-how lie right here.

Since your emotions, goals, and movements drift out of your charge judgments, preserving close tabs on them, especially in case you take a look at the stoic quality of conquering illogical emotions and impulses, is essential. Keeping a near eye on your choices is like getting a regular have a look at of your technique performance. The signs and symptoms and symptoms of terrible settings and feelings may be diagnosed, and countermeasures can be taken to prevent a full-blown emotional or behavioral outburst.

Thus a ways, we've got got placed that the disciplines and virtues of Stoicism, just like the traditional ideals of Stoic teachings, are continuously interconnected and overlapping. In unison, they aid in non-public development and progress closer to lifestyles in tune with nature and others. You can achieve eudaimonia with the resource of the usage of this issuer.

Chapter 10: Integrating Stoicism Into Modern Society

We want to all don't forget how we better incorporate Stoicism into modern-day-day day manner of life. Stoicism is a philosophical manner of lifestyles that dates once more many centuries. The institutional resurgence of Stoicism in our day may be traced to the permeability of expertise, the breakdown of socialist structures, and the universality of stoic doctrines.

You can also additionally examine extra in every week than the not unusual man or woman back then discovered out in an entire 3 hundred and sixty five days. Suddenly, some aspect that befell in a bit village have become worldwide facts. Life is so complete of obstacles that tenacity and self-cognizance are required for fulfillment. Everyone aspires to reap their entire capability and take rate in their destinies. Stoicism is a method for purchasing there.

Until currently, many individuals must go to established organizations for steering whilst making lifestyles's most vital selections. Schools, church houses, and the circle of relatives unit are examples. The manner of modernization has had various results at the framework of those establishments. Based for your values, you can find that plenty of these establishments aren't relevant or as beneficial as they as speedy as were.

Knowledge and facts may additionally additionally want to handiest be determined at educational institutions and libraries. They cannot compete with the Internet, and lots of have needed to merge their structures into it. But, more is needed to vicinity them earlier of the opposition. Yet, the Internet can be used to find out credible assets of statistics in addition to unreliable ones.

A huge percent of the population now not regularly attends religious services. Many folks who attend church now not depend upon important lifestyles selections at the teachings or mandates of the religion. The church's significance in lots of humans's lives has been referred to as into doubt in present day years. The dynamics internal families have also shifted. Single-discern families, same-intercourse parenting, and one of a kind varieties of circle of relatives shape had been uncommon inside the past however at the moment are increasingly not unusual.

With all of the global exchange changing the social canvas, it is simple to get swept up in its maelstrom. As a cease result of the virtual revolution, our society has long gone through profound adjustments in modern years. In the face of all this upheaval, modern Stoicism also can assist us keep our composure.

Unlike superb philosophical schools, Stoicism is meant to be practiced rather than studied. Here are three suggestions that let you advantage your aim:

Strive to stay a virtuous life

Living a existence of kindness, generosity, and goodwill towards others is what we suggest while we communicate of virtue. For stoics, this is the holy grail. If you want to be virtuous, you need to discover ways to carry out the wonderful in yourself in any state of affairs, actual or terrible. Maintaining intellectual clarity is essential for success. When confronted with a morally grey situation, it's vital to count on how your best self, or the person you recognize, could act.

Strive for lengthy-term improvement

One precept of Stoicism is a strength of will to gradual growth. It's about empowering you to enhance as a person any further. Generally talking, historical stoics had been extra open to developing adjustments to instances that others could see as not feasible.

The idea of neuroplasticity, which Seneca alludes to in this instruction, is relevant to modern society. Sustainable improvement includes making dreams to emerge as a better person than you had been the previous day and following thru on the ones efforts each day. This moreover explains the Navy SEAL motto: The best clean day modified into the day past.

Peaceful coexistence with others

People are the middle of our life. Indeed, it sums up what it method to be part of a network and a society. You have to talk with and paintings with human beings with reviews and beliefs at odds at the side of your non-public. In Stoic philosophy, the importance of family and pals is paramount. Living a fruitful and non violent existence is a capability you may collect through Stoicism.

The standards outlined above led Stoics hundreds of years ago and stay crucial now.

You can also learn how to be resilient in the face of problem and reach most, if no longer all, of your life desires by the usage of manner of adopting the concepts of Stoicism.

When became the ultimate time you concept approximately why you need to examine Stoicism? Things have no longer gone as planned greater instances than you want to recollect. It hurts while lifestyles unexpectedly is going in a extraordinary direction from the handiest you had deliberate. Being denied some aspect you want or have prepared for is probably annoying, however it is a crucial a part of lifestyles. A person's existence can be grew to become the wrong way up at the same time as a string of misfortunes leaves them feeling like no longer anything will ever move right.

Your life may additionally moreover best wreck you if you have a guiding idea. Stoicism is better than different ideologies like epicureanism and hedonism as it does not interest on elements outdoor to your existence, which might be regularly past your control. There's no requirement for formal schooling or an reputation of different cultures to exercising Stoicism, making it a remarkable deal extra useful in regular lifestyles.

Stoic conviction includes many things, but having a sturdy internal middle of control is excessive on the list of priorities. This is the conviction that no person but you may make certain happiness or distress. Hence, you haven't any proper to quote your upbringing, youngsters, or every other factors as an excuse for failing. The factor of residing is continuously to push yourself to enhance your general performance. What plans do you have were given if anything horrible have been to upward thrust up these days? Your response to the complexity or worry of your function. Find the motivation, zeal, and strength you want to conform to your lifestyles. Everyone people is responsible no longer best for our deeds but moreover for the emotions we unfold to others.

In order to live the stoic lifestyles to the fullest, you need to cultivate an inner middle of manipulate. You may additionally moreover furthermore take stock of the outdoor elements influencing your life. Anything that isn't always inner your head is considered outside. Sickness, your employment, the conduct of others, the climate, or perhaps politics also can all fall below this elegance. Detachment from the outside, strength of will and intellectual calm are the quality gear for managing the stresses of the outside international. You can also choose that the weather be colourful in area of wet and dreary, however you furthermore mght distance your self from this simply so your lifestyles is unaffected irrespective of the weather. You increase the functionality to truely receive anything takes place. Rather than wallowing in helplessness and self-pity, you are taking price of your scenario and appearance forward constructively.

Death is each different outside difficulty that has a considerable impact on our lives. Death is an unavoidable truth of life. Many people are scared of it, but they can't get away it. We spend our complete lives gaining knowledge of the manner to live and live to tell the tale. In hindsight, we spend our whole lives identifying the way to die. The finality of mortality catches many people off defend due to the reality they have now not made the most of their time.

Nobody is aware about at the same time as they'll die, however you could have an concept when it is coming near. People who have led widespread lives are commonly unshaken via way of the threat of loss of life because of the fact they anticipate they've got lived their best lives. Longevity on my own is not any guarantee of happiness, opposite to commonplace notion.

The idea of demise is normally beside the point to our every day life. Many human beings waste their lives away doing no longer a few aspect due to the fact they neglect approximately dying as some component that doesn't have an effect on them, simplest to recognize their futility in the end. Be as thoughtful as possible, and deal with every day as although it have been your remaining on Earth, the usage of your ideals and brilliant efforts to the entirety you do.

The nice approach to residing a stoic lifestyles is to attempt to be an excellent person. What does it recommend to come to be virtuous? How can one expand a extremely good moral character? How do you incorporate this into your ordinary lifestyles? These easy inquiries can exchange your existence in strategies you may in no way have imagined. It have to help in case you lived through a set of pointers. How do you address setbacks and issues in lifestyles? How do you act within the presence of your bosses and/or subordinates?

Make non secular vicinity part of your every day recurring. Stick with some detail idea you decide to pursue. Your efforts to become a higher man or woman want to advantage no longer excellent your self but moreover others round you.

Contemporary Stoics' Guiding Principles

The ancient Greeks positioned a excessive price on pursuing happiness and decided it in Stoicism. Stoicism is a practical manner of dwelling. It is sometimes misinterpreted as being equal to being emotionally unavailable. Nonetheless, it has formerly been installed to be a satisfying manner of existence. An historical philosophy that has helped many exchange their lifestyles perspectives and discover achievement.

Practicing Stoicism can also help you turn out to be more attuned to the first-rate factors of existence, which includes gratitude, contentment, and happiness. It is based totally totally on which include rate in all factors of your life and attention. The exercising of Stoicism may additionally moreover boom the nice of your existence in masses of techniques. Several present day-day packages of stoic philosophy might be cited underneath. This teaches you realistic programs to help you dive deeper into your persona to find out extra approximately your self and the way to be resilient and adapt better to ordinary troubles.

Attitude Is Everything

It is difficult to adjust subjects over which you haven't any manipulate. On the alternative hand, your mind-set is some element you could adjust, and it's miles in doing so that you will find out your actual power. Stoicism is predicated carefully on one's capacity to be present and aware. It allows you end up greater aware of yourself and your environment. Being aware allows you understand the instances over that you have an effect on and those you do not. It's pointless to expend highbrow assets on being indignant about belongings you can't trade. The greater you recollect issues, the much more likely you're to create them.

As you train to be stoic, you discover ways to strengthen your thoughts against the stresses of existence that you cannot alternate. Here, we can use a well-known Buddhist story approximately Buddha and his foe Mara to provide an explanation for. When Mara found of Buddha's talents, he despatched an military to kill him. The military became to begin with tasked with throwing flaming boulders within the direction of Buddha, however as soon as they approached their purpose, they transformed into vegetation and dropped to the ground.

Mara, angry, gave orders for his guys to update to arrows. Similarly, whilst the arrows approached Buddha, they transformed into plant life and plopped on the ground. Buddha had discovered out to guard his happiness from out of doors affects so Mara could not hurt him.

In this fable, the fiery rocks and arrows constitute unsightly occurrences and bad thoughts to your lifestyles. These are uncontrollable outdoor elements. What you could do about them is alter your attitude. Adopting a more fantastic outlook may furthermore transform your mind into a peaceful stronghold, unfastened from the detrimental affects of bad thoughts and behaviors. Protecting your self from out of doors impacts requires mastery of your emotions, reactions, and angle.

Beware of the Materialistic Society

The scale of capitalism inside the globe now could be unfathomable. In every path you bypass, someone is trying to sell you some thing. As a stop give up result of our in no manner-completing want for consumer goods, capitalism is given an additional boom. The hassle with materialism is that we stay in a way of existence that fosters preference in preference to achievement and happiness.

The scourge of consumerism is the normal stress to adopt new models. Our every day publicity to higher gadgets further drives this through social media and marketing. This constant bombardment of suitable photographs may additionally additionally result in an awful cycle of searching an increasing number of.

You can constantly do higher than what you currently have access to. You empty your pockets at the cutting-edge day devices. At the same time, you without difficulty convince your self that you may be satisfied, content material material cloth, and fulfilled with the resource of that item, however this revel in best lasts till the new edition is out. Most people do not care as lots about being the primary to get some factor as they do approximately making sure all people is privy to they have it and could in no way forget approximately that they had been the number one. Stoics purpose to need masses a good deal much less. Reduce your choice thru attempting much less. Learn to understand the little subjects in lifestyles. You apprehend its without a doubt worth and charge due to the manner it benefits you.

Put Your Words to Work

According to Epictetus, "Don't provide an explanation for your philosophy. Embody it." One need not be a stoic to understand the significance of this announcement. Everyone values deed greater than phrases, no matter in that you adventure. The stoic view is that everybody need to take duty for their movements. The duty to your personal thoughts and deeds lies most effective with you. But it would not mean you have to usually be too essential of your self. It is rather encouraged that you overtly renowned and take shipping of your moral duties.

The gold large route of movement in any given situation need to be cautiously considered before being taken. Do higher if you could. Do your great to decorate, every in terms and deeds. Your mind need to encourage your acts to the volume that they assist you benefit fantastic function, the very nice benefit inside the stoic manner of life.

Seek Real Happiness

Real happiness is a few issue that arises from the indoors. It is actual and unbiased of a few thing else to your lifestyles. You rate even the maximum mundane sports, which includes buying water from a vending device. You do no longer should wait until you are in a situation in which you can not get bottled water to realise how vital it's miles.

According to stoic philosophy, your stage of happiness is independent of outside conditions. That is what proper happiness is all about. When happiness is intrinsic, one is unfazed by way of way of way of outside situations due to the truth they've got already skilled more than enough.

Setting oneself up for disappointment is as smooth as trying extra than what this lifestyles has to provide. Does this propose that stoics cannot take pleasure in the equal pleasures that the rest people take as a right however can handiest discover happiness within the business enterprise of different satisfied humans? No. The excessive lifestyles remains inside your obtain. The one key distinction is which you need to keep in mind a few component aside from high-priced an absolute need for contentment. You should be glad with or without them.

Accepting Loss in Life

Many human beings's dissatisfaction with their existence stems from an insatiable want for delivered. Gratitude is the important thing to your contentment. Acknowledge and rate the humans which is probably already on your lifestyles. The excellent way to understand what you have were given is to image your self without it. Being thankful for what you have enables you to revel in it more absolutely.

We don't provide a 2nd idea to many things in our lives for the reason that we take them as a right. We anticipate they need to be in our lives, but we address them complacently as an alternative. When we act as even though things ought to be ours, we omit out on that they'll be now not ours to have. Consider how disheartening it'd be to observe of the dying of a close to buddy first factor in the morning. While it hurts, picturing your life with out your buddy might probable make you recognize them greater. You price them greater now that you've had a while to reflect.

In planning for the destiny after a loss, it is vital to place most effective a bit inventory at the subjects you currently private, as the following day is in no way promised. According to Stoic philosophy, you have to find out happiness, calm, and tranquillity on your possessions. Putting all your eggs in a single basket might be disastrous because of the reality you in no manner apprehend whilst the out of doors element will pass. Rather than feeling sorry or sad over losing something outside, you want to be happy approximately the opportunity to have owned and used it within the first region.

Understand the way to Establish Internal Goals

One Stoic precept you have to get preserve of is the externality of times. According to this philosophy, you should in no way allow outside sports to disrupt your balance.

Things like health, net page site visitors, and lousy weather fall below this magnificence. You constantly ruminate approximately those subjects. These are usually one of the first topics humans have a have a observe once they upward push up inside the morning. You cannot live your life with out them. Going out with out checking the climate forecast may want to in all likelihood damage your day if you did now not prepare for the afternoon rain.

You should moreover exercising distancing yourself from the outcomes of activities, specifically the ones you mistakenly do not forget to be indoors your manipulate. If you're working a agency, stay targeted and anticipate your undertaking will thrive because of your know-how and industrial organization expertise. Your employer's success or failure is past your manipulate.

The analogy of a rugby suit enables make clean this factor. You may installation a goal of prevailing to your very own motives.

Maybe your squad has prepared nicely all week; the alternative organization is vulnerable. It seems which you may emerge powerful. Sadly, the destiny of that in shape can also be determined with the aid of using a plethora of various factors that you likely need to have taken into consideration.

The first mystery is the rugby ball itself. After bouncing as soon as at the floor, its next landing spot is certainly random. Second, you still want to take into account the weather. The winds may also flip in competition to you. A moist pitch might likely make it tough to your players to work collectively. You can also even undergo injuries to as a minimum one or greater of your key gamers or absolutely have absolutely considered one of in recent times at the same time as your opponent has researched your procedures in advance of time and appears to have a reaction for each assault. If triumphing changed into your critical purpose going into the sport, then any deviation out of your plan is probably to go away you feeling pissed off.

Certain subjects can't be controlled, however that doesn't recommend you must no longer try to make a difference. This consists of that specialize in subjects you have got final control over, which incorporates your moves.

Many out of doors affects affect the final product. As a result, your desires ought to be based on efforts you can manage. As an possibility to seeking to win the in shape, you can instead attention on improving your diploma of education and training. Encourage your squad to offer their all on the arena. Doing the whole thing efficiently and but losing is irritating, but there can be now not a few factor you may have carried out in a distinct manner.

Always aim to be the maximum organized you may be. Don't float right proper right into a activity interview looking earlier to you will receive the manner. Instead, make sure you could solution any questions articulately thru getting prepared well, dressing effectively, and rehearsing thoroughly. It wasn't purported to be yours if you though failed to gain the mission.

The most obvious gain of adhering to this rule is that it enables you turn right into a better man or woman. The simplest subjects that should be tied to the goals you installation for your self are your very very very own mind-set and attempt. Learn to break up yourself from the final results as it is not yours to offer.

Your lifestyles might be higher in case you placed stoic ideas into exercise every day. Stoicism has the advantage of no longer being an absolute philosophy with an all-or-not something mind-set. It's as much as you to determine the way you want your lifestyles to move from proper right here on out. You might also moreover pick out which additives of Stoicism to encompass and, most probable, add more over time. If you can preserve your moves, reactions, and thoughts-set underneath test, you may quickly learn how to be thrilled about your conditions and find out the satisfaction lifestyles gives.

Chapter 11: Material Possessions

Materialism is a fashion of life that prioritizes bodily comfort above private and non secular values. We carelessly use the phrase "having an excellent time" without expertise the intensity of which means it conveys. "having an great time" is regularly used loosely to justify ignoring one's obligations or giving in to one's egotism.

Many human beings inside the contemporary international strive for self-sufficiency to recognise their pastimes. Given our questioning ability, know-how, and energy, modern society frequently encourages us to rely upon the monetary blessings of utilising our abilities. Much of the regulations of our contemporary lives are set via our desires for wealth. We've gotten to the level in our society wherein we prioritize our dreams above our wishes via usually seeking out new and higher ways to meet the ones desires.

The pursuit of cloth devices has been hypothesized to contribute to unhappiness. It's paradoxical, thinking about that monetary prosperity frequently grows swiftly inside the identical duration. Saddeningly, many individuals miss out on how their obsession with coins contributes to a miles large trouble. The amount of cash you may amass to your lifetime is unbounded. Your preference to increase your riches, energy, and fortune drives you to work extra and take extra risks.

Constant publicity to famous lifestyle and on-line social networks conditions us to location a top elegance on cloth possessions. Wherever you pass, you may see classified ads promising you the arena via imparting you with the correct element to decorate your life, whether or not or not or now not it's miles making you happier, wealthier, or greater famous. Everyone is so centered on making upgrades to themselves that they forget about the opportunity individual and what they will be going thru. The amount of advertising messages transmitted in a unmarried day is top notch, but entrepreneurs accomplish their cause on the give up of the day. Constant bombardment with messages may also make you bear in thoughts giving their objects a attempt. That's the point at that you sincerely lose it.

How does materialism function? Employing the identical tactic, advertisers want to steer you to shop for their gadgets through way of creating you enjoy lousy approximately no longer doing so. They persuade you that you honestly want their services or products and that you are lots worse off without it. They make you sense lousy, a good way to sell you some aspect to make you experience higher. They prey on susceptible humans through the use of using their emotions.

The price at which your happiness is being eroded with the aid of immoderate consumption is quicker than you may say your complete call backward. Most of lifestyles's requirements are, sadly, monetary. The pursuit of economic achievement is not inherently horrible. Attaching an excessive amount of in fact well worth to topics that can be offered with coins is what eats away at your happiness. What do you sense at the same time as you apprehend that a person else has them and you do not, or while you apprehend that they have got a superior version of what you do have? That's why you feel a good deal much much less and masses much less glad.

The prolonged-term, obsessive pursuit of financial fulfillment harms your intellectual fitness. Financial setbacks may undermine your feeling of safety in existence, decrease yourself-admire, and make you experience inept. When human beings's charge variety are in disarray, they regularly retreat from friends and social sports activities due to the reality they no longer sense like they belong.

Stoicism and Minimalism

The thoughts of Stoicism also can additionally assist you live a more easy lifestyles and get away the grip of consumerism and materialism in notable, now not in fact via education you to live with less. The goal of the minimalist way of existence is to simplify one's life just so one can also furthermore commit one's time and energy to what surely subjects and makes one glad. Many who have struggled beneath the load of consumerism usually record feeling at peace, having a experience of success, and experiencing happiness after transitioning to minimalism. The independence acquired thru a reduction in possessions is useful. Reducing useless possessions can will will let you provide interest to what is in fact important. This makes it easier to be pleased about what one has in preference to continually searching greater.

It's crucial to apprehend that minimalist living does now not want to give up all your possessions or restricting how you spend your effort and time. The cause of this exercising is to make you more thankful for what you have already were given. Is proudly proudly owning a Tesla going to make you happier than you have been earlier than? You can despite the fact that buy adorable jewelry and live on the seashore. Do it if you may find the money for to and can make it show up. What counts is if it brings you serenity and makes you glad.

Happiness is a personal experience; what makes you glad won't make someone else happy. In maintaining with our earlier instance, even though a Tesla might also want to make you satisfied, a Prius would probably make someone else happy. So, minimalism isn't involved with what you do but with how and why you do it. It's a lifestyle in that you consciously lessen your fabric possessions to the naked minimum. You care plenty less approximately particular human beings's views and what they endorse you to do, and alternatively, you become greater aware about what you need.

In the following detail, we're capable of check a few critical stoic teachings approximately materialism that you could probably positioned into effect for your life.

Value within the Fundamentals

Pursue calm and relaxation with the resource of manner of limiting your activities to the bare minimum. As a give up result, you could maintain your electricity for the subjects that absolutely depend. When you do not must reputation on little topics, you could provide your entire interest to enhancing the subjects that virtually count.

Recognizing what subjects maximum permits you to devote time and electricity to it. Priorities also can moreover inform you masses approximately who you are and wherein your values lie. You've come to understand that your priorities, in location of your out of doors look, display the proper nature of who you're. The perspectives and judgments of others aren't as huge as your non-public persona.

It's satisfactory to peer the results of your hard art work repay. You can change your car, cloth dresser, preferred hairstylist, perfume, and lots of others. This new look would possibly in all likelihood offer you with a experience of improved recognition. Nevertheless, the ones changes are just superficial. The pleasant alternate that honestly counts is the simplest you're making at the internal in view that it's the best one that could have an impact on you, and fine you can ever understand about it.

Inward adjustments are extra important on the grounds that they have charge.

Your person reveals plenty approximately your personality. Individuals' personalities may be inferred no matter how they pick out out out to get dressed. People can inform because of the manner you behave every day. Everyone receives 24 hours to do some factor they want. As mentioned in advance than, de-cluttering your existence and focusing your efforts in which they will do their fine are crucial minimalism standards. There are numerous opportunities for the present day stoic to unique their particular abilities and develop as humans. Make use of them to enhance yourself in widespread ways. You want to but prioritize growing your abilities and one-of-a-kind hobbies similarly to assembly your everyday responsibilities. Those who exercising present day Stoicism get recognition and which means from their lives through focusing on what topics most to them.

You Should Count Your Blessings

Do now not restore your thoughts on belongings you do now not very own, wishing they have been yours. Concentrate on your possessions alternatively. Christian hymn "Count Your Blessings" also can moreover come to mind. You can be shocked at sincerely how masses things you very personal in case you truely completed an inventory. If you did not already have it, how plenty might you want it and be inclined to fight for it?

Following Stoic philosophy teaches you to overcome the temptation to hoard and be pleased approximately what you have got. Besides that, you want to learn how to distance your self from your material property emotionally. No day goes through with out as a minimum one man or woman weighing their fortunes in competition to the ones of some distinct. That makes no feel. It's a stressful game without a result in sight. Remember that the character you are attempting to keep up with can be doing the identical detail. Even worse, they will not moreover be your combatants. They may additionally need to have enough money to stay lavishly due to the fact that's what they need to do.

Having more stuff does not make you any satisfied or higher. That fake enjoy of contentment will only cause more material accumulation. Your existence might be filled with fear and misery ultimately. Look at what you have in place of what distinct people have. You must price these gadgets greater now because of the strive you install prolonged in the beyond.

Moreover, stoic philosophy emphasizes that you do not non-public the assets you very very own. You rapid borrowed them from the universe, and the universe may also without troubles take them decrease again.

Recognize the superb matters on your existence, however recognise they is probably taken away. Keep your thoughts at peace by means of using fending off living at the possessions of others or evaluating your self to others.

Value Cannot Be Found in Materialism.

Possessions might probable appear like everything and extra, however this isn't always the case. You must, however, not be apathetic approximately fabric objects. Stoicism holds that the maximum vital topics are those you could manage, together with your personal mind and deeds. They are indicative of who you're as a person. Everything out of doors your mind and behaviors need to be independent because of the fact you can't manage them. As a give up result, you might be an terrific or terrible man or woman primarily based totally honestly to your thoughts and deeds in preference to what others bear in mind you.

Nonetheless, it's miles in our human nature to have wonderful impartial options. They encompass companionship, amazing look, cash, delight, and unique health. Intuitively, all of us charge health and wealth extra especially than the opposites. But, irrespective of how masses you want the ones items, you have not any manipulate over them. They are beside the point because of the truth you cannot control them. Whatever conditions you discover your self in, the actions and thoughts you're taking are the maximum critical additives of your life.

As a result, Stoics are unconcerned with material gadgets. You do now not personalize subjects too much or allow them to have an effect in your feelings. The problem with fabric belongings is which you emerge as resistant to trade while you get associated with them. This is due to the fact letting pass can be uncomfortable or maybe painful. As a cease quit end result, you start to revel in worthless and unhappy in case you ever need to element with any of your stuff. Realizing which you do now not have any control over your possessions may additionally moreover help you undertake a greater minimalist lifestyle.

What Do You Need in Life?

We regularly overestimate the importance of the gadgets we need for a satisfied life. Stoic philosophy, at the same time as stripped of its remarkable trappings, teaches that the everyday character has few wishes effortlessly met on a small price range. No recollect in which it comes from, the primary cause of food and water is to meet your urge for food and thirst, respectively. Clothing need to maintain you warm, and your home ought to preserve you secure from inclement climate.

Most individuals can count on having a roof over their heads. Our simple wishes are generally met. If you placed yourself within the footwear of a homeless individual for each week, you can rapid find out how little you actually need to get through the usage of. You do no longer must skip outdoor every. Imagine in that you have been in existence or three years in the past. You have been all proper regardless of getting fewer property than you've got have been given in recent times. While your flat become smaller and your income become decrease, you have been content on the side of your lifestyles. Now that you've made it, you understand your preceding achievements had been no longer enough. After the development, you may desire even more.

It's ok to desire extra so long as you do not lose sight of what you actually need. The thriller to happiness is distinguishing between what you want and need. Do you, as an instance, care extra approximately carrying comfortable and embossed shoes with a famous logo name? How many do you need, , four, or six? Avoid falling victim to the purchase paradox, wherein your choice for some issue is powerful however simplest lasts till you got it, after which you want something else. The cutting-edge-day stoic knows the difficulty of handling cloth possessions. You recognize what you want and how crucial it's far in your life. Your life revolves across the pursuit of goals rather than a costly.

The Art of Minimalism

The key is to analyze in which to attract the street. Stoics rate simplicity in lots of elements, together with not actually their possessions however moreover their interactions. When one speaks excessively, maximum of what's stated is useless. This is sound advice, given that many humans in modern way of life are seeking out the subsequent massive little little bit of buzz. Stop and maintain in mind whether or no longer some factor definitely ought to be said or completed earlier than you're announcing or do it. You have no enterprise corporation sharing it if this isn't always the case.

Many subjects must be spoken approximately. You have seen to your contacts with others that humans often say silly matters to appear smart, humorous, or hip. Some people intentionally damage social norms to advantage splendor into a selected organization. Learn to be quiet and pay hobby cautiously in preference to rambling on about not anything of importance. Listening actively and deciding on up on inferences is a essential elements of powerful communique. You discover ways to be aware of nonverbal cues like posture, eye contact, and motion that complement what is being spoken.

\

www.ingramcontent.com/pod-product-compliance
Lightning Source LLC
Chambersburg PA
CBHW071447080526
44587CB00014B/2021